THE PIP

ANTHOLOGY OF WORLD POETRY OF THE 20TH CENTURY

VOLUME I

*Edited with a Preface
by Douglas Messerli*

EL-E-PHANT 1

GREEN INTEGER
KØBENHAVN & LOS ANGELES
2000

GREEN INTEGER BOOKS
Edited by Per Bregne
København/Los Angeles

Distributed in the United States by Consortium Book
Sales and Distribution, 1045 Westgate Drive, Suite 90
Saint Paul, Minnesota 55114-1065
and in England and the Continent by
Central Books
99 Wallis Road, London E9 5LN
(323) 857-1115/http://www.greeninteger.com

First edition published 2000
Copyright ©2000 by Douglas Messerli
All permissions for the publication of poetry appear
at the end of each poet's section of this book.
Back cover material ©2000 by Green Integer
All rights reserved.

Cover Design: Douglas Messerli
Photographs: left to right, top to bottom
Rocco Scotellaro (drawing from *Ommagio a Scotellaro*, Leonardo Mancino, ed.);
Ingeborg Bachmann (by Kuno Raeber); Rubén Darío; Jorge Guillén;
Gunnar Eckelöf (drawing by Gunnar Brusewitz); Ágnes Nemes Nagy;
Frigyes Karinthy; João Cabral de Melo Neto; Osip Mandelshtam
Typography: Guy Bennett

LIBRARY OF CONGRESS CATALOGING IN PUBLICATION DATA
Messerli, Douglas, ed. [1947]
The PIP Anthology of World Poetry
of the 20th Century
Volume 1
ISBN: 1-892295-47-4
p. cm — Green Integer
I. Title II. Editor — Douglas Messerli

THE PIP ANTHOLOGY OF WORLD POETRY
OF THE 20TH CENTURY
VOLUME I

Green Integer
6026 Wilshire Boulevard
Los Angeles, California 90036

(323) 857-1115 FAX: (323) 857-0143
E-Mail: djmess@greeninteger.com
Visit Our Web-Site: www.greeninteger.com

Douglas Messerli, Publisher

TABLE OF CONTENTS

Preface / Douglas Messerli   7

Rafael Alberti [Spain]   9

Ingeborg Bachmann [Austria]   23

Rubén Darío [Nicaragua]   31

Günter Eich [Germany]   37

Gunnar Ekelöf [Sweden]   49

J.V. Foix [Spain]   59

Ángel González [Spain]   67

Jorge Guillén [Spain]   77

Hagiwara Sakutarō [Japan]   84

Hayashi Fumiko [Japan]   95

Frigyes Karinthy [Hungary]   104

Artur Lundkvist [Sweden]   109

Jackson Mac Low [USA]   116

Osip Mandelshtam [Russia]   125

João Cabral de Melo Neto [Brazil]   133

Henri Michaux [Belgium]   144

O.V. de Milosz [Lithuania/France]   154

Ágnes Nemes Nagy [Hungary]   161

Amelia Rosselli [Italy]   169

Rocco Scotellaro [Italy]   177

Takahashi Mutsuo [Japan]   183

Index   196

PREFACE

The first volume of *Poems for the Millennium*, published in 1995 by the University of California Press and edited by my friends Jerome Rothenberg and Pierre Joris, in its often brilliant gathering of many poets previously unknown to American audiences, greatly moved me and increased my already high respect for its editors. But at the same time, I found that volume and the second often frustrating because of whom it had not included and its lack of more detailed biographical and bibliographical information. Clearly it was the best collection of international writing in English to date, but there were such important innovative poets missing! Both my positive and negative reactions led, I believe, to good results. I had already determined to edit my own international volume, and had begun spending one day each week in the University of California, Los Angeles Research Library researching and reading new work. Of course, as a publisher, I had the good fortune of having none of the page limitations and other restrictions which any editor must face when undertaking such a project; arbitrarily I determined that my selection would consist of two or three volumes of about 1,200 pages each, similar in size and perspective to the anthologies of American poetry and drama, *From the Other Side of the Century* I and II, I had previously edited.

I truly enjoy working in libraries and am proud of my ability to uncover little known or obscure works. But over the months even I was amazed at the wide range of truly innovative poetry I was experiencing just by scanning the stacks. Certain poets led me to other poets; reading in certain languages introduced me to other poets in that language; and serendipitous discoveries brought me an ever increasing body of wonderfully inventive writing. Increasingly it became apparent just how little American readers—including myself—knew about international poetry. While my poet friends and I each knew several figures from major langugues, most of us knew little of the startlingly fresh writing of, for example, Turkey, Romania, Uganda or Martinique. Before long I had developed a working list of about 370 poets whom I felt I *had* to include; and since I had pre-determined to incorporate brief biographies, full listings of books in the original language with place of publication and date, and about ten pages of poems for each poet, my concept of three volumes of 1,200 (the largest size book my printers can accommodate) was erroding. Moreover, as I began to write for permissions (knowing that this would be an impossibly complex process both in terms of ordering the research and the financial resources if I did not spread this out over several years), I gradually began to perceive the immensity and, perhaps, impossibility of such a project. But what a joy it was reading all of these works!

Out of my enthusiasm and attempts to share the writing I was discovering I created an international committee of poets to serve as advisors to what I called The Project for Innovative Poetry, dedicated to presenting and promoting internationally innovative poetic writing. P I P (the acronym for this project) began its own journal, *Mr. Knife, Miss Fork.* My publishing house, Sun & Moon Press, and my personal imprint, Green

Integer, both began publishing more and more volumes of international poetry. I was possessed.

However, as the years passed, despite my payments for rights, the actual publication of the large anthologies seemed further and further away. Finances for such literary publications were drying up nationally; and a grant request for the first volume from the National Endowment for the Arts was turned down. Accordingly, Sun & Moon Press received no Endowment monies in 1998.

Late that year, I perceived that I would have to reenvision my project if I wanted to see it come to life. Perhaps, I reasoned, if I published many smaller volumes instead of three or four omnibus ones, I would be better off. At first I conceived these as clothbound research tools; I wrote to the reference departments of hundreds of university and college libraries, but I received little response. Finally, in mid-1999 I determined to proceed with the first of these smaller volumes, the one you now hold in your hands, published in a popular paperbound edition, which is still useful as a research tool. I shall follow with volumes of approximately the same size every season until I have completed publishing my list of poets. Providing that I uncover no further poets—a dreadful concept—I should be finished in about eight years! Each volume, representing poets throughout the century from various languages, will be arranged alphabetically and will contain an index of poets included in all previous volumes of the series.

My goal is to bring to public attention—both through individual sales and through library reference—the work of major international poets, hopefully sharing my sense of discovery and wonderment at the wide range of poetic expression through the century, and to send readers to the original or translated texts. If I have learned nothing else from this enjoyable task it is that poetry, no safely contained mode of expression, throughout the world in the 20th century has been an energetic and often uncontrollable beast of language upon whose back the reader is taken to worlds that exist only in thinking itself.

Such grand efforts are always the work of many. I would like to thank the staffs of the University of California Research Library and the University of California, San Diego Geisel Library. As always, Diana Daves was a remarkably patient and observant editor and proofreader, supported by Thérèse Bachand and Jacy Young. Guy Bennett's typographic skills coupled with his editorial and linguisitic abilities were central to this project. Numerous friends, Charles Bernstein, Jerome Rothenberg, Pierre Joris, Marjorie Perloff, Paul Vangelisti, Luigi Ballerini, Will Alexander, and others must be thanked for their help and suggestions. I toast all the many translators and editors of the books included—to the new millennium!

Rafael Alberti [Spain]
1902–1999

One of the major poets of the Generation of 1927, Rafael Alberti was born in Puerto de Santa María, Spain. In 1917 he moved with his family to Madrid, where he began as a painter, working in both the impressionist and cubist styles. He was awarded the highly regarded National Literature Prize for his very first collection, *Marinero en tierra* (1925). Nostalgic in its tone, this collection has a great deal of youthful exuberance, and the nostalgia was less apparent in his next publication, *La amante* (The Mistress), printed in 1926. It was only with his 1927 collection *El alba del alhelí* (The Dawn of the Wallflower), however, that he pushed for more complex linguistic patterns that characterize so much of his later writing. The style of *Cal y canto* of 1929, cast in a more baroque manner, reaches its highest expression in *Sobre los ángeles* (*Concerning the Angels*) of the same year. In this collection Alberti expresses his own spiritual crisis in terms that are universal, which established him as an internationally important writer.

In 1939 he was exiled to the United States, but continued to keep close personal and poetic connections with Spain, and after Franco's death in 1977, he returned to his homeland. Alberti has produced over fifty books of poetry, as well as several plays.

BOOKS OF POETRY:

Marinero en tierra (Madrid: Biblioteca Nueva, 1925); *La amante: Canciones* (Malaga, 1926); *El alba del alhelí* (Santander: Ediciones para Amigos de J. M. de Cossío, 1927); *Sobre los ángeles* (Madrid: CIAP, 1929); *Cal y canto* (Madrid: Rivista de Occidente, 1929); *Consignas* (Madrid: Octubre, 1933); *Un fantasma recorre Europa* (Madrid: La Tentativa Poética, 1933); *Poesía 1924–1930* (Madrid: Cruz y Raya, 1934); *Verte y no verte* (Madrid: Aguirre, 1935); *13 bandas y 48 estrellas* (Madrid, 1936); *Poesía 1924–1937* (Madrid: Signo, 1938); *Poesía 1924–1938* (Buenos Aires: Losada, 1940); *Entre el clavel y la espada 1939–1940* (Buenos Aires: Losada, 1941); *Pleamar 1942–1944* (Buenos Aires: Losada, 1944); *A la pintura: Cantata de la linea y del color* (Buenos Aires: Lopez, 1945; revised edition: Buenos Aires: Losada, 1948); *Antologia poética 1924–1944* (Buenos Aires: Losada, 1945); *Poesía 1924–1944* (Buenos Aires: Losada, 1946); *El ceñidor de Venus desceñido* (Buenos Aires: Botella al Mar, 1948); *Coplas de Juan Panadero (Libro I)* (Montevideo: Pueblos Unidos, 1949); *Buenos Aires en tinta china* [edited by Attilio Rossi] (Buenos Aires: Losada, 1951); *Retornos de lo vivo lejano 1948–1952* (Buenos Aires: Losada, 1952; revised edition, Barcelona: Libres de Sinera, 1972); *Ora marítima* (Buenos Aires: Losada, 1953); *Baladas y canciones del Paraná* (Buenos Aires: Losada, 1954); *Diez liricografías* (Buenos Aires: Bonino, 1954); *María Carmen Portela* (Buenos Aires: Losada, 1956); *Sonríe China* (with María Teresa León) (Buenos Aires: Muchnok, 1958); *Cal y canto, Sobre los ángeles, Sermones y moradas* (Buenos Aires: Losada, 1959); *El otoño, otra vez* (Lima, 1960); *Los viejos olivos* (Caracas: Dirección de Cultura y Bella Artes, 1960); *Poesías completas* (Buenos Aires: Losada, 1961); *Poemas escénicos* (Buenos Aires: Losada,

1962); *Diez sonetos romanos* (Buenos Aires: Bonino, 1964); *Abierto a todas horas 1960–1963* (Madrid: Aquado, 1964); *El poeta en la calle: Poesía civil 1931–1965* (Paris: Globe, 1966); *Poemas de amor* (Madrid: Alfaguara, 1967); *Roma, peligro para caminantes 1964–1967* (Mexico City: Mortiz, 1968); *Libro del mar*, edited by Aitana Alberti (Barcelona: Lumen, 1968); *Poesía anteriores a Marinero en tierra 1920–1923* (1969); *Los 8 nombres de Picasso, y No digo más que lo que no digo 1966–1970* (Barcelona: Kairós, 1970); *Canciones del altro valle del Aniene, y otros versos y prosas 1967–1972* (Buenos Aires: Losada, 1972); *Poesía* (Madrid: Aguilar, 1972); *Poemas del destierro y de la espera*, edited by J. Corredor-Matheos (Madrid: Espasa Calpe, 1976); *Poesía* (Havana: Arte y Literatura, 1976); *Coplas de Juan Panadero 1949–1977, seguida de Vida bilingüe de un refugiado español en Francia 1939–1940* (Madrid: Mayoría, 1977); *Poesía 1924–1977* (Madrid: Aguilar, 1977); *El matador: Poemas escénicos 1961–1965* (Barcelona: Seix Barral, 1979); *Fustigada luz (1972–78)* (Barcelona: Seix Barral, 1980); *Canto de siempre* (Madrid: Espasa Calpe, 1980); *101 Sonetos (1924–75)* (Barcelona: Seix Barral, 1980); *Versos sueltos de cada día (1979–82)* (Barcelona: Seix Barral, 1982).

ENGLISH LANGUAGE TRANSLATIONS:

Selected Poems, translated by Lloyd Mallan (New York: New Directions, 1944); *Selected Poems,* edited and translated by Ben Belitt (Berkeley: University of California Press, 1966); *Concerning the Angels,* trans. by Geoffrey Connell (London: Rapp and Carroll, 1967); *The Owl's Insomnia,* edited and translated by Mark Strand (New York: Atheneum, 1973); *The Other Shore: 100 Poems,* edited by Kosrof Chantikian, trans. by José A. Elgorriaga and Paul Martin (San Francisco: Kosmos, 1981); *Concerning the Angels,* trans. by Christopher Sawyer-Lauçanno (San Francisco: City Lights Books, 1995); *To Painting,* trans. with an Introduction and Notes by Carolyn L. Tipton (Evanston, Illionis, 1997).

The Cruel Angels

Birds, blind beaks
of that time.
Pierced
by a zealous red wire,
by the voice and the capricious will,
long, short, of their dreams:
the sea, the fields, the clouds,
the tree, the thicket…
Blind, dead.

Fly!
"We can't.
How are we supposed to fly?"

Gardens that were the air
of that time.
Canes of nocturnal rage,
spurrings of the torpid,
turbid winds,
that would be leaves, flower,
that want…
Gardens of the south, laid waste!
Of the south, dead.

Take the air!
"We can't.
How are we to take the air?"
In your hands,
still hot from that time,
wings and leaves, dead.

Let's bury them.

–Translated from the Spanish by Christopher Sawyer-Lauçanno

(from *Sobre los ángeles*, 1929)

False Angel

That I might pass through the knot of the tuber,
the worm's habitation of horn,
and hear out the crackle and rasp of a world
and bite on the petrified starlight, false angel,
you have set up your booths for the bypasser west of my dream.

You who ride my identical tides,
urged by a star's fall, yoked to a common betrayal, who see me
and listen: withdraw to the desolate voice in the ruins.
Hear the patience of stone crossing over toward death.

Do not break from the keep of those hands!

The spider fails, far from his web,
the ivy leaf bursts into flame and rains blood at the touch of a shoulder.
Moonlight shines through the bones of the lizard.
For all we remember of heaven,
the cold's rage will stiffen the edge of the thorn
or work in a fraudulent furrow
to strangle the last consolation of morning: the birds.
Those who ponder the living will encounter the muddy devices
of false and implacable angels,
somnambulist angels who keep watch on the stations of sloth.

What has it profited you?
The dankness lies close to the glass and beads to a point,
a nightmare of frost awakens the spike
and the scissors to freeze in the scream of a crow.

It is finished.
You have labored for nothing in the stale of a comet's explosion,
and murdered the murdered,
and spoken grief's longitude in a deathwatch for shadows,
and pressed for the death rattle there in the capes of the air.

—*Translated from the Spanish by Ben Belitt*

(from *Sobre los ángeles,* 1929)

The Dead Angels

Search for them; search for them there
in the drainpipe's forgotten insomnia,
gutters blocked by a silence of garbage.
Where the puddle goes blank to the clouds:
the eye's devastation,
a ring that is broken,
a star trodden under.

I have seen them before:
revelations of rubbish that flash from the mist.
And touched them myself:
dead clods come to nothing, a downfall
of tiles from the tower and the barrow.
Under the chimney's debris, the print
of the leaf on our boot soles, there is nothing.

Nothing to hope for.
Only vagabond parings that go out with no flame,
desolation that batters old furniture
near the names and the symbols that grow cold on the walls.

Search for them, search for them there:
under the wax that buries the word on the page,
the name in the angle of notepaper
in the dust-devil's swirl.
There, by the bottle ignored in the grass,
the shoe sole lost in the snow,
the rust of the razor blade left on the edge of the precipice.

—*Translated from the Spanish by Ben Belitt*

(from *Sobre los ángeles,* 1929)

Soul in Torment

That soul in its torment, alone,
that soul in perpetual hurt, pursued
by a dead incandescence.
By a death.

Latches and doorways and passkeys
spring open to startle us.
Curtains of frost grown immense in the night,
subtle as vapor,
catch, kindle,
and lengthen.

I know you:
I remember you,
lackluster candle, hoar halo, spent nimbus.
You, my assailant, however enfeebled in wind.

A vigil of eyelids
descends on our world.
The lash of the earthquake despoils what we dreamt
and temblors demolish the stars.
The whole havoc of heaven and the trash of this world,
a rubbish of feathers and viols, the psaltery's string
and a boneyard of angels.

No one shall enter: no thoroughfare into that heaven.

Tormented, tormented forever,
a spirit in torment.
Always in counter-light,
overmasterd by none and alone,
most lonely of spirits.

The bird strives with the ship,
and the man, with the rose,
sorties and routs in the wheatfields,
an explosion of blood in the breakers.
And the fire.
The slaughter of fire,
a dead incandescence
always watchful in shadow.

A soul in its torment:
the dead incandescence
your undoing.

—*Translated from the Spanish by Ben Belitt*

(from *Sobre los ángeles*, 1929)

Open Letter

...There are fish that bathe in sand
And cyclists that run the waves.
I think of myself—at school upon the sea.
Infancy now on boat, now bicycle.

Free world, the first balloon floated
Over the spiral shriek of freighters.
Carthage face to face with Rome,
Their sandals ready for setting sail.

At ten years of age no one tastes of Latin;
And Algebra, who ever heard of it?
Or chemistry, or Physics. My God!
The sun itself was hunted in a hydroplane.

...And open-air movies. Anne Boleyn, dressed
Unexplicably in blue, walks along the shore;
If she's not discovered by the sea, a cop
Dissolves her in the flower of his flashlight.

Gangsters in dress-suits before my eyes
Their pistols point. While arrested
They're swept soullessly away from me
In skies of sudden cities, which I alone spied.

New York may be seen in Cadíz, or in the Port;
Seville may be in Paris, Iceland or Persia.
A Chinaman is not Chinese. A passerby may be
White or equally black and green.

Everywhere, you, from your rose,
Ticketless, from your motionless center,
Dumb-tongued, rule supreme, king of everything…
Because the world is a picture postcard album.

Multiplied, you pass by on the wind,
On the flight of train or tram;
The lightning of your thoughts within never dies
But dies instead a million moons removed from your lips.

I was born with the movies, heaven help me!
Under a net of 'planes and cables,
When the stately coaches of kings were done
And the Pope climbed into an auto.

From the skies I saw, like blue angel feathers,
The showers of telephone messages falling;
The seraphic orchestras of the air
Crashed from headphones through the catacombs of my ear.

Fish from the clouds, of canvas and nickel,
Drop in the sea newspapers and letters.
(These postmen do not believe in sirens
Nor in the waltzing waves, but in death.

And still bald heads are faded in the moon
And tearful hair pressed within books.
A stowaway of snow whitens the shadows,
Committing suicide in gardens.

What is to become of my soul which long has been
Playing the continuous record of absence.
What of my heart that no longer leaps,
Offended by both chance and accident?)

Search my eyes and, lost, they'll wound you
With longing like all shipwrecked things,
The bulk of Norths now defunct,
The lonely staggering of seas.

Casques of gunpowder and sparks, horsemen
Without courage or a mount among the wheat;
Basilicas of debris, erected spouts of fire,
Blood, lime and ashes.

But also, a sun in each arm,
An aviatrix dawn, a golden fish,
With written initial and number on her forehead
And in her beak an unstamped letter of blue.

Messenger—the electrical voice and hind-end—
Of the hurrying heavens,
Of the confines of love, of the crackle
Of the world's mechanical rose.

Know me, who sent to all mankind
Over the telephone my dynamic madrigal:
"What are you made of, steel, tin and lead?"
One more flash of lightning, and the new life begins.

—*Translated from the Spanish by Lloyd Mallan*

(from *Cal y canto*, 1929)

Buster Keaton Searches Through the Forest for His Sweetheart, a Full-Blooded Cow (A Poem for Recitation)

1, 2, 3, and 4.
Four footprints. My shoes won't fit them.
If my shoes won't fit them,
Then whose tracks are they?
A shark's,
A new-born elephant's, a duck's?
Perhaps a flea's or quail's?

(Tweet, tweet, tweet.)

Georginaaaaaa!
Where are you?

I can't hear you, Georgina!
What will your papa's mustachios
Think of me, Georgina?

(Paaapaaaaa!)

Georginaaaaa!
Are you there or not?

Birch-tree, where is she?
Where is she, Alder-tree?
O Fir-tree, tell me where is she?

Has Georgina gone by here?

(Tweet, tweet, tweet.)
She did pass, at one o'clock, chewing grass.
Cawkoo,
The crow was luring her with a mignonette.
Caw caw,
The owl with a dead she-mouse.
Forgive me, gentlemen, but I feel the need to weep!
(Wah-wah, wah-wah!)

Georgina!
Now you lack just one horn
To acquire a postman's cap and a doctorate degree
In the truly useful profession of cyclist.

(Beep-beep, beep-beep.)

Even the crickets pity me;
And the tick shares my grief and anguish.
Pity him who looks for you and weeps for you
In evening clothes among the soft rains;
In derby hat who tenderly fears for you
Through blade by blade of grass.

Georginaaaaaaaaaaaaa!

(Mooooo.)

Are you a lovely lass
    or a full-blooded cow?
My heart always told me
    you were a full-blooded cow.
And your papa said you were a lovely lass.
A full-blooded cow.
A lass.

A cow.
A girl or a cow?
Or—a cow and a girl?
I never did know anything.
                    Adios, Georgina.
                        (Boom!)

(1929)

—*Translated from the Spanish by Lloyd Mallan*

Goya

Sweetness, rape
laughter, violence,
smiling, blood,
gallows, the fair.
A tortured demon with a knife
chases the light & the darkness.

        Your eye: I keep it in the fire.
        Your head: I nibble on it.
        Your humerus: I crackle it. Your harrying
        inner ear: I suck its snail.
        Your legs: I bury you up to them
        in mud.
                One leg.
                Another.
                        Flailing.

        Run away! But stay
        to witness, to die
        without dying.

O light of the infirmary!
The blind circle of gaiety.
Histrionic agony.
When everything falls down, slips back,
and ridiculous Spain swerves off the track,
and a broom flaps away.

Flying.
The devil, breasts of an old woman.
And the torero,
Pedro Romero.
In bloodied yellow,
Pepe-Hillo.
And the reverse
of the Duchess' obverse.
Her Majesty the Grotesque
with His Majesty the Grotesque.
And the prowess
of the hand of the Holy Office.
And the persecution
of that scare-crowed
execution.
The stout
& big-nosed Cardinal:
Snout.
And the Meadow below the rose skies.
And the man in the top-hat,
darkly wrapped up to his eyes.
The disgrace of grace,
& the grace of disgrace.
And the poetry
of a painting of light
& a work of the night.
And the greak mask
in flight,
gone off
to dance in the procession.

The great mask, death,
the Royal Court, need,
vomiting, the nightly round,
satiety, black hunger,
the long-horned Goat, the dream,
peace, war.

Where do you come from, strange creature, percipient goat
with upward-snaking horns
& chestnut coat?
Where to you come from, funeral,
fetus,

unreal nonsense
nonetheless true,
sketchings, etchings,
deepest
cobalt blue,
clouds of rose-milk,
thicket of trees,
sun-shading
silk, silk
blithe as breeze?

> Little hobgoblins. Informers.
> Get going, they're waking up.
> They say "yes" & give their hand
> to the first man who comes by.
> Now is the hour.
>   Let us rejoice!
>   Bon voyage.
> Dream of the lie.
>   And a burial
> that truly terrifies the countryside.

Painter: throughout your endless years,
may Grace remain in tears
and Horror smile.

—Translated from the Spanish by Carolyn L. Tipton

(from *A la pintura*, 1948)

Ingeborg Bachmann [Austria]
1926–1973

Born in Klagenfurt, Austria on June 25, 1926, Ingeborg Bachmann studied law and philosophy at the universities of Inssbruck, Graz, and Vienna. She received her degree from the University of Vienna for a dissertation on Heidegger in 1950.

Bachmann's first poetry was published in *Lynkeus, Dichtung, Kunst, Kritik,* edited by Hermann Hakel, while she was attending the university. After her graduation, she went on to become a scriptwriter at Radio Rot-Weiß-Rot in Vienna. During these years she traveled to Munich to read at the influential gathering of post-war German poets known as Gruppe 47, an appearance arranged by the poet Paul Celan, whom she had met in Vienna. The reading was highly lauded, and the next year, 1953, Backmann received the Gruppe 47 Prize for her first collection, *Die gestundete Zeit (Borrowed Time).* The wide success of that book led to requests for poems, radio plays, and opera libretti, a great number of which she produced over the next several years.

The same year as her award, Bachmann moved to her beloved Italy, first to the island of Ischia, and then to Naples and Rome, where she remained until 1957. In 1955 she also traveled to the United States at the invitation of the Harvard Summer School of Arts and Sciences, led by Henry Kissinger. The following year her second volume of poetry, *Anrufung des Großen Bären (Invocation of the Great Bear)* was published. As a result she was asked to deliver the inaugural lectures for the poetry chair founded at Frankfurt University in 1959, helping to assure her recognition as the most important German poet since Gottfried Benn. The same year she was awarded the prestigious Bremen Literature Prize.

During the late 1950s she continued to work in radio and television, now as dramaturge for Bavarian Television and Radio in Munich and Hamburg. But in 1958, she moved to Zürich, becoming involved with the Swiss author Max Frisch until 1962, when she returned to Rome. Her 1960 libretto for Hans Werner Henze's opera *Der Prinz von Homburg* and her 1961 collection of short stories, *Das dreißigse Jahr* brought her further acclaim. She was awarded the Georg Büchner Prize in 1964 and the Austrian State Prize for Literature in 1968. In 1971 Suhrkamp Verlag published her novel, *Malina.* Bachmann's collection of short stories, *Simultan* (R. Piper Verlag) was published the following year. On September 26, 1973, Bachmann fell asleep in her Rome apartment while, apparently, smoking a cigarette in bed. The fire department found her unconscious and badly burned. She died three weeks later, on October 17th, at the age of 47.

BOOKS OF POETRY:

Die gestundete Zeit (Frankfurt: Frankfurter Verlaganstalt, 1953; Munich: Piper, 1957); *Anrufung des Großen Bären* (Munich: Piper, 1956); uncollected poetry published in *Werke* [4 volumes] (Munich: Piper, 1978).

ENGLISH LANGUAGE TRANSLATIONS:

Songs in Flight: The Collected Poems, translated and introduced by Peter Filkins, with a Foreword by Charles Simic (New York: Marsilio Publishers, 1994).

Paris

Lashed to the wheel of night
the lost ones sleep
in the thunderous passages beneath;
but where we are, is light.

Our arms are full of blossoms,
mimosa from many years;
goldness showers from bridge after bridge
breathless into the stream.

Cold is the light,
still colder the stone before the gate,
and the basins of fountains
are already half empty.

What will happen if we, homesick
and helpless with windblown hair,
remain here and ask: what will happen
if we survive the test of beauty?

Lifted onto the wagon of light,
and waking, we are lost
in the alleys of brilliance above;
but where we are not, is night.

—Translated from the German by Peter Filkins

(from *Die gestundete Zeit*, 1953)

Wood and Shavings

Of hornets I will say nothing,
since they are so easy to spot.
Also, the current revolutions
are not that dangerous.
Death has always been resolved
in the fanfare of noise.

Yet beware the May flies and women,
beware the Sunday hunters,
beauticians, the undecided, the well meaning,
the ones devoid of contempt.

Out of the forests we carried branches and logs,
and for a long time there was no sun.
Intoxicated by paper on the conveyer belt,
I no longer recognize the branches
or the moss, dyed in darker tints,
or the word, carved into the bark,
impudent and true.

Wasted paper, banners,
black posters... By day and by night
the machine of faith rumbles beneath
this or that star. But in wood,
as long as it is still green, and with gall,
as long as it is still bitter, I am
willing to write what happened at the start!

Make sure you stay awake.

The swarm of hornets chases the shavings
blown by the wind, while at the fountain,
resisting the curled allure
that once made us weak,
my hair bristles.

—*Translated from the German by Peter Filkins*

(from *Die gestundete Zeit*, 1953)

Early Noon

Silently the linden greens in approaching summer,
far from the cities there glimmers
the pale brightness of the day moon. Already it's noon,
already a sunbeam flashes in the fountain,
already the fabulous bird's flayed wing
lifts itself beneath the rubble,
and the hand that's cramped from casting stones
sinks into the budding corn.

Where Germany's sky blackens the earth,
its beheaded angel seeks a grave for hate
and offers you the bowl of the heart.

A handful of pain vanishes over the hill.

Seven years later
it occurs to you again,
at the fountain before the portal,
don't look too deep within,
as your eyes fill with tears.

Seven years later,
inside a mortuary,
the hangmen of yesterday
drain the golden cup.
Your eyes lower in shame.

Already it's noon, in embers
the iron bends, on the thorn
the flag is hoisted, and onto the cliff
of the ancient dream the eagle is welded,
remaining forever.

Only hope cowers, blinded in the light.

Throw off its shackles, help it
down the slope, cover
its eyes so that
the shadows don't scorch it!

Where Germany's earth blackens the sky,
a cloud seeks words and fills the crater with silence
before summer is made aware of its sparse rain.

The unspeakable passes, barely spoken, over the land:
already it's noon.

—*Translated from the German by Peter Filkins*

(from *Die gestundete Zeit*, 1953)

Tell Me, Love

Your hat tips slightly, greets, sways in the wind,
your uncovered head has touched the clouds,
your heart is busy elsewhere,
your mouth takes on new tongues,
the quaking-grass is growing fast,
summer blows asters to and fro,
blinded by tufts you lift your face,
you laugh and cry and fall to pieces,
what will become of you—

Tell me, love!

The peacock spreads its tail in festive wonder,
the dove lifts high its feathered collar,
bursting with coos, the air expands,
the drake cries, the whole land eats
wild honey, while in the tranquil park
each flower bed is edged with golden dust.

The fish blushes, overtakes the school
and plunges through grottoes into the coral bed.
To silver sand music the scorpion shyly dances.
The beetle scents his mate from afar;
if only I had his sense, I'd also feel
wings shimmering beneath her armored shell,
and I'd take the path to distant strawberry patches!

Tell me, love!

Water knows how to speak,
a wave takes a wave by the hand,
the grape swells in the vineyard, bursts and falls.
The guileless snail creeps out of his house.

One stone can soften another!

Tell me, love, what I cannot explain:
should I spend this brief, dreadful time
only with thoughts circulating and alone,
knowing no love and giving no love?
Must one think? Will one not be missed?

You say: another spirit is relying on him...
Tell me nothing. I watch the salamander
slip through every fire.
No dread haunts him, and he feels no pain.

—*Translated from the German by Peter Filkins*

(from *Anrufung des Großen Bären*, 1956)

Black Waltz

The oar dips at the sound of a gong, the black waltz starts,
with thick dull stitches, shadows fall upon guitars.

Beneath the threshold, in a mirror, my dark house floats,
the flaring points of light now softly radiate out.

Hanging above the sounds: the harmony of waves in motion,
always the the surface shifts towards another destination.

I owe the day its market cries and blue balloon—
stone torsos, the whirling flight of birds, the *pas de deux*

that they perform each night, silently turned towards me,
Venice, on pylons and floating, East and West in harmony!

Only mosaics strike roots and hold fast to the ground,
about a buoy—pillars, frescoes, and grimaces spin around.

There never was an August that saw the lion's sun,
for its mane was set adrift when the summer had begun.

Consider idolatrous light, the claw marks on the bow,
and in the wake of the keel, the carnival masks in tow,

as over the flooded plaza, to the tower, sails a garment,
also the brackish water, as well as love and its scent,

the introduction, a prelude to stillness, not another beat,
the oar that's striking intervals and the coda of the sea!

—*Translated from the German by Peter Filkins*

(from *Anrufung des Großen Bären*, 1956)

A Type of Loss

Commonly used: seasons, books and music.
The keys, the tea cups, the breadbasket, sheets
    and a bed.
A dowry of words, of gestures, brought along,
    used, spent.
Social manners observed. Said. Done. And always
    the hand extended.

With winter, a Vienna septet and with summer I've
    been in love.
With maps, a mountain hut, with a beach and
    a bed.
A cult filled with dates, promises
    impossibly given,
enthused about Something and pious before Nothing,

(—the folded newspapers, cold ashes, the slip of paper
    with a jotted note)
fearless in religion, as the church was this bed.

From the seascape came my inexhaustible painting.
From the balcony, the people, my neighbors,
    were there to be greeted.
By the fire, in safety, my hair had its most exceptional
    color.
The doorbell ringing was the alarm for my joy.

It was not you I lost,
but the world.

—Translated from the German by Peter Filkins

(uncollected 1964-1957, from *Werke*, 1978)

PERMISSIONS

"Paris," "Wood and Shavings," "Early Noon," "Tell Me, Love," "Black Waltz," and "A Type of Loss"
Reprinted from *Songs in Flight: The Collected Poems*, translated and introduced by Peter Filkins, with a
Foreword by Charles Simic (New York: Marsilio Publishers, 1994). Copyright ©1994 by Peter Filkins. Re-
printed by permission of Marsilio Publishers.

Rubén Darío [Félix Rubén García Sarmiento] [Nicaragua] 1867–1916

The lack of parental concern in his childhood, his first wife's early death, and an unhappy marriage to his second wife, resulted in sense of moral anguish throughout much of Rubén Darío's life and writing. This, coupled with his sensuality constantly in opposition to his fervent faith in Roman Catholicism created, in many of his works, a tension between the sacred and the profane.

Traveling from 1886–1889, Darío visited outlying areas of his own country, Chile, Guatemala and other Central American countries. He also traveled, in 1892, to Spain as a member of Nicaragua's commission to the Quadricentennial Celebration of the New World's discovery. He also visited New York and Paris (in 1893), Argentina (in 1893–98), and European countries (1898–1915).

Among Darío's early literary mentors was Francisco Gavidia of El Savador, who introduced him to French literature, especially the work of Victor Hugo; and Eduardo de la Barra and Pedro Balmaceda (the latter the son of Chile's president) of Chile. Through these individuals, Darío encountered current French books and reviews.

In 1888 he published *Azul* (Blue), which after a review by the Spanish poet Juan Valera, brought him international attention, and a recognition of Darío's involvement with modernism. While in Buenos Aires in the late 1890s, serving as Colombia's consul, Darío co-founded, with Ricardo Jaimes Freyre, the magazine *Revista de América*, the first symbolist review in the Hispanic world. While in Argentina, he also published the Verlaine-inspired *Prosas profanas y otros poemas* (1896, *Profane Hymns and Other Poems*, 1922) and *Los raros*, a volume of essays.

Cantos de vida y esperanza of 1905 (Songs of Life and Hope) is considered one of his major works. Here, Darío has abandoned much of the French imagery of his previous books and replaced it with strong new world imagery and subjects.

Darío also wrote short stories, philosophical essays, and other works. He died at the age of 49, in 1916.

BOOKS OF POETRY:

Abrojos (Santiago de Chile: Imprenta Cervantes, 1887); *Rimas* (Santiago de Chile: Imprenta Cervantes, 1887); *Azul* (Valparaíso: Imprenta y Litografía Excelsior, 1888; Madrid: Espasa-Calpe, 1984); *Prosas profanas y otros poemas* (Buenos Aires: Imprenta Pablo E. Coni e Hijos, 1896; second ed. Paris-México: Librería de la Vda. de Ch. Bouret, 1901); *Cantos de vida y esperanza. Los cisnes y otros poemas* (Madrid: Tipogr. de la Revista de Archivos, Bibliotecas y Museos, 1905); *Oda a Mitre* (Santiago de Chile: Imprenta A. Eymeoud, 1906); *El canto errante* (Madrid: M. Pérez Villavicencio Editor, 1907); *Poema del Otoño y otros poemas* (Madrid: Biblioteca Ateneo, 1910); *Muy antiguo y muy moderno* (Madrid: Biblioteca Corona, 1915); *Obras completas* (Madrid: Mundo Latino, 1917-1919); *Baladas y canciones* (Madrid: Biblioteca Rubén Darío Hijo, 1923);

Sonetos (Madrid: Biblioteca Rubén Darío, 1929); *Obras poéticas completas* (Madrid: Aguilar, 1932); *En busca del alba* (Buenos Aires: Arístides Quillet, 1941); *Brumas y luces* (Buenos Aires: Ediciones Argentinas S.I.A., 1943); *Quince poesías* (Barcelona: Argos, 1946); *Poesís completas* (Madrid: Aguilar, 1952)

ENGLISH LANGUAGE TRANSLATIONS:

Eleven Poems, trans. by Thomas Walsh and Salomón de la Selva (New York: Putman, 1916; revised as *Eleven Poems of Rubén Darío* [New York: Gordon, 1977]); *Selected Poems of Rubén Darío*, trans. by Lysander Kemp (Austin: University of Texas Press, 1965).

from *Thistles*

I

First, a look;
then the burning touch
of hands; and then
the racing blood
and the kiss that triumphs.
Later, night and delight. Later, the flight
of that craven gossip
seeking another victim.
You are right to weep, but it is too late!
Do you see? I told you!

XII

I would not want to see you a mother,
my dark sweet woman.
But then, there is a canal
not far from your house,
and of course it is well known
that man is not born with the knowledge
of how to swim.

—*Translated from the Spanish by Lysander Kemp*

(from *Abrojos,* 1887)

Towers of God! Poets!

Towers of God! Poets!
Lightning rods of Heaven
that resist the fierce storms
like solitary mountains,
like peaks in the wilderness!
Breakwaters of eternity!

Magic hope foretells

the day when the traitorous siren
will die on her musical rock.
Hope! Let us still hope!

Still hope. The bestial element
consoles itself with its hatred
of blessèd poetry, hurling
insults from race to race.

The rebellion from below
is against excellence.
The cannibal waits for his chunk of flesh
with red gums and sharpened teeth.

Towers, fasten a smile to your banner.
Confront this evil and suspicion
with a proud puff of the breeze
and the tranquillity of the sea and the sky —

—Translated from the Spanish by Lysander Kemp

(from *Cantos de vida y esperanza*, 1905)

To Roosevelt

With a Hebrew prophet's voice or a verse from Walt Whiman,
Is how we must approach you, hunter!
Primitive yet modern, simple yet complex,
With one part Washington and four parts Nimrod,
You are the United States,
You are the future invader
Of that ingenuous America of native blood,
That prays to Jesus still and still speaks Spanish!

You are proud and strong and typical of your race;
Cultured and clever, firmly opposed to Tolstoy.
In breaking horses and in killing tigers
You are an Alexander-Nebuchadnezzar.
(You are a professor of the Active Life,
As fools say nowadays.)

You hold that life is a fire,
And progress an eruption;

That where your guns can reach,
There you control the future.
        No.

   The United States indeed are great and powerful:
They shake themselves, and a deep tremor rocks
The enormous ridges of the Andes to their base.
Once Hugo said to Grant: "The stars are yours."
(For, rising but then, the sun of the Argentine
Scarcely shone; the Chilean star had barely risen...)
You're rich; to that of Hercules you join the cult of Mammon;
And, illumining the path that leads to easy conquest,
Liberty rears her torch above New York.

   But our America, in which from the far-off days
Of Netzahualcoyotl poets have sung,
Which still preserves the footprints of great Bacchus,
And learned long since the alphabet of Pan,
Which reads the stars, and knew the great Atlantis
Whose fame resounding reaches us from Plato;
This, our America, from the first has lived, and lives
On light and fire, on perfume and love,
The land of Moctezuma, of the Inca,
Fragrant still with the memory of Columbus,
America Catholic, America Spanish,
America in which the noble Guatemoc said:
"I'm on no bed of roses,"; this America,
That rocks with hurricanes, and lives by love,
O men of Saxon eyes and barbarous souls, she lives,
Dreams, loves, vibrates, is daughter of the Sun;
Beware, for Spanish America still lives;
The Spanish Lion has a thousand cubs.
You need, O Roosevelt, to be, for God himself
The terrible rifleman, the strong hunter
To keep us in your iron grasp.

   Everything is yours,
you think: but you still lack
— God!

    —Translated from the Spanish by G. Dundas Craig, with revisions
      by Douglas Messerli

(from *Cantos de vida y esperanza*, 1905)

Philosophy

Welcome the sun, spider, no need for spite.
Give thanks to God, o toad, for your life.
The hairy crab carries rosy thorns
and the mollusk something similar to the female sex.

Learn to be what you are, enigmas, given form
Give up the Norm,
a responsibility, in time, passed on to the Divine.
(Play, cricket, to the moonshine, and bear, dance.)

       —*Translated from the Spanish by Douglas Messerli*

(from *Los cisnes y otros poemas*, 1905)

Life and Death

Who proffers us the goblet brimming?
Who gives us the hidden star?
Who gives blood to the Tree of Abundance?
    Life.
Who sees that we drain the fragrant cup?
Who detains the steps of luck?
Who is it who all hope perverts?
    Death.

      —*Translated from the Spanish by Gilbert Alter-Gilbert*

(from *Poesís completas* [previously uncollected], 1952)

Günter Eich [Germany]
1907–1972

Born in Lebus an der Oder, in eastern Germany, in 1907, Günter Eich was one of the major post-war figures of Germany poetry and radio.

In 1918 his family moved to Berlin; eight years later, Eich graduated from a gymnasium in Leipzig and began studying Chinese at the University of Berlin. In 1927 he transfered to the Leipzig University, where he joined his interest in sinology to economics. In the year 1929–1930 he took courses in sinology at the Sorbonne in Paris, and continued his studies in economics, without completing his degree.

His involvement in lyric poetry began at the University of Berlin, and it was there, with Martin Raschke, he wrote his first radio play. From that period until the outbreak of World War II, he was involved with Berlin Radio.

During the war Eich served on the Russian front, and was taken prisoner by the Americans in 1945. In the P O W camp he continued his lyric writing. Upon his release he settled in Bavaria, joining, the following year, the now famed Gruppe 47 (Group 47), a loose association of postwar German authors. In 1950 he won the Gruppe 47 prize for his radio play "Geh nich nach El Kuwehd!" ("Do Not Go to Kuwait").

His first postwar poetry collections were published in 1948 and 1949. *Abgelegene Gehöfte* (Remote Farmsteads) and *Untergrundbahn* (Subway) both perfectly captured the sentiments of postwar Germany, a country in chaos and deprivation. Eich's writing, while at times highly lyrical, also contained a keen sense of observation and wit that exposed hyprocisy and easy answers. His poem "Inventory" was among the most popular postwar poems.

In 1953 he married the German writer Ilse Aichinger. His most important collection, *Botschaften des Regens* (Messages of the Rain) was published in 1955; once again Eich took experiences from everyday life and infused them with a great sense of mysteriousness and wonder. His later work moved toward a more pessimistic view of human race, and, at the same time, a fragmentation of lyrical forms. The pattern of his poetry once again suited the period of rebellion against the older generation, and made Eich a popular poet among younger readers as well.

At the time of his death in 1972, he was living in Gross-Gmain, Austria.

BOOKS OF POETRY:

Gedichte (Dresden: Jess, 1930); *Abgelegene Gehöfte* (Frankfurt am Main: Schauer, 1948); *Untergrundbahn* (Hamburg: Ellermann, 1949); *Botschaften des Regens: Gedichte* (Frankfurt am Main: Suhrkamp, 1955); *Zu den Akten: Gedichte* (Frankfurt am Main: Suhrkamp, 1964); *Anlässe und Steingärten: Gedichte* (Frankfurt am Main: Suhrkamp, 1966); *Maulwürfe: Prosa* (Frankfurt am Main: Suhrkamp, 1968); *Ein Tibeter in meinem Büro: 49 Maulwürfe* (Frankfurt am Main: Suhrkamp, 1970); *Gesammelte Werke*, edited by Ilse Aichinger, Susanne Müller-Hanft and others [4 volumes] (Frankfurt am Main: Suhrkamp, 1973); *Gedichte*, selected by Ilse Aichinger (Frankfurt am Main: Suhrkamp, 1973)

ENGLISH LANGUAGE TRANSLATIONS:

Günter Eich, translated by Teo Savory (Santa Barbara, Californa: Unicorn, 1971); *Valuable Nail: Selected Poems of Günter Eich*, translated by Stuart Friebert, David Walker, and David Young (Oberlin, Ohio: Oberlin College, 1981)

Inventory

This is my cap,
this is my coat,
here's my shaving gear
in a linen sack.

A can of rations:
my plate, my cup,
I've scratched my name
in the tin.

Scratched it with this
valuable nail
which I hide
from avid eyes.

In the foodsack is
a pair of wool socks
and something else that I
show to no one,

it all serves as a pillow
for my head at night.
The cardboard here lies
between me and the earth.

The lead in my pencil
I love most of all:
in the daytime it writes down
the verse I make at night.

This is my notebook,
this is my tarpaulin,
this is my towel,
this is my thread.

—Translated from the German by David Young

(from *Abgelegene Gehöfte*, 1948)

Where I Live

When I opened the window,
fish swam into the room,
herring. A whole school
seemed to be passing by.
They sported among the pear trees too.
But most of them
stayed in the forest,
above the nurseries and the gravel pits.

They are annoying. Still more annoying
are the sailors
(also higher ranks, coxswains, captains)
who frequently come to the open window
and ask for a light for their awful tobacco.

I'd like to move out.

—*Translated from the German by David Young*

(from *Botschaften des Regens,* 1955)

End of August

With white bellies the dead fish hang
among duckweed and bulrushes.
The crows have wings, to fly away from death.
Sometimes I know that God
cares most about the existence of the snail.
He builds her a house. Us
he does not love.

Evening: the bus drags
a white banner of dust
as it brings home the soccer team.
The moon glows among willows
reconciled with the evening star.
How near you are, Immortality,
in the wing of a bat,
in the eyes of those headlights
coming down the hill.

—*Translated from the German by David Young*

(from *Botschaften des Regens,* 1955)

Munch, Consul Sandberg

The possibility
that the world is composed of colors
fills me with contempt.
I wish I had invented ice
and the boiling point
of metals.
Look at me:
I stand on your canvas
a nightmare of confidence
success in trouserlegs
and pointed boots;
the comedies of death
are played for my amusement.
In my mouth
I've got spit
for your hopes.

—*Translated from the German by David Young*

(from *Zu den Akten*, 1964)

For Example

For example sailcloth.

Translating one word into one other word,
that takes in salt and tar
and is made of linen,
preserves the smell,
the laughter and the last breath,
red and white and orange,
time controls
and the godly martyr.

Sailcloth and none,
the question:
where's an interjection
as an answer.

Between Schöneberg
and the star cover
the mythical place
and stone of meadows.

Task, set
for the time after you're dead.

—Translated from the German by Stuart Freibert

(from *Zu den Akten*, 1964)

A Mixture of Routes

1

The forests in the glove compartment,
random cities,
promise of food and lodging.

My cortisone face
shoved across pastures,
my electroshock,
my cozy motel.

Unnatural pleasures
happily practiced,
having lived with
the wise ciphers of the timetable,
on my mapped tongue I keep
these lands for my own.

2

Ach: that is aqua
and it's a sigh.
Go into the seas!

Get, unwittingly,
to Kagoshima,
the first city,

unwittingly to the sighs
of asylum doors,
the waters around tanneries,

fishkitchens
south of the Main,
the peevish, red

parking lights,
a dateline
in Obergries,

a sixth-form
gym class,
a farewell ball

with the girl named Tabe
and the elevator girls
whom nobody looks at,

get there
to say Adieu
get to stationery stores and

a middlesized ferryboat

3

Finally the doors are closed,
the taps shut off,
ashes in the oven, nothing left,
we can go.

Always the narrow passes, the snow tongues,
where are the roses of the teacher,
the rain-animals through broken windows,
the movie programs through the letter-slot
on Thursdays.

Where are, after the snow tongues,
after Thursdays, our
ways? Into the forest toward Hiroshima,
between dogs the stairs in the quarry,
a moment of comfort drawn from barracks,
from rotting grass, rotting ropes.

—Translated from the German by David Young

(from *Anlässe und Steingärten*, 1966)

Continuing the Conversation

1
Remembering the dead man

I observed
that remembering is a form of forgetting.

It said:
rescue the flames from the ashes,
pursue Geology in the discarded
sediment of the instant,
restore the time sequence
from the insoluble chemistry.

It said:
separate the critique of birdflight
from the morning shopping
and the expectation of love.
Proceed to where
the parallels cross.
Fulfill the demands of logic
by means of dreams.
Take the fossils from their cases,
thaw them with the warmth of your blood.
Seek the sign
instead of the metaphor
and thereby the only place
where you are, always.
I move along
in order to translate anthills,
to taste tea with a closed mouth,
to slice tomatoes
under the salt of the verses.

2
Invite him over

The shame, that the survivor is right,
exempt from sentencing
and with the arrogance of judgment!

Who denies
that green things are green?
That lends our word
a lovely security,
the significance of a solid base.
But the stylizing
that the heart
imposes on itself
keeps its motives
like the ammonite
the dead man looks at.
It wants to extend feelers,
turn vine-leaves into fernspirals,
bring errors into blossom,
hear autumn as a whiff of snow.

But don't forget the houses
in which you live among us.
The lounge chair in the garden
will suit you
or the view of trees through the window
that makes you prop
your elbows on your knees.
Come in out of the rain, and speak!

3
Converse with him

Here it began and it didn't begin,
here it continues
in a noise from the next room,
in the click of the switch,
in shoes taken off behind the door.
The pallor of your face
that blots out colors
isn't valid now.
Sentences come from habits
that we scarcely noticed.
The way the necktie's tied
is a momentous objection,
the ability to fall asleep quickly
a proof against subjective interpretations,
the preference for tea
classifies the existence of animals.

4
Find his theme

Interchangeable:
the knocking at the door
which began the conversation
and the waving
as the streetcar clanged,
the name on the grave cross
and the name on the garden gate,
children grown up
and postcard greetings from Ragusa.

Words as pulsations of air,
the organ note from the bellows,
the decision
to hear the song
or to be the song—
warped uprights
to the fall line of phosphorus,
when the theme begins.
No variations accepted
not the excuses of power
and the reassurances of truth,
use cunning
to track down the questions
behind the answer's broad back.

5
Reading his book and his death

Figures settled in
at the shut-down mines of Zinnwald
behind the demon frenzy
of subalpine slopes and season,
while the foreground
is occupied by ruffians
who divide our hours among themselves.

Pirna in balance with the Pyramids,
the freedom of express trains
cashed in small change by block leaders,
the family ethically founded,

contempt for nomads and loners.

But the objections
come back to the sentences
like eager adjectives,
a line of termites
that hollows them out
to a thin skin
of black letters.

The Style is Death,
the shot in the stomach,
white rose in a morhpine dream,
jokes to amuse life,
salvos into a snowstorm.

6

Winning confidence from his life

While you share the thoughts,
direct the conversation by your death,
writing along on poems,
gathering pears
and viewing new landscapes
(but I finally
resisted garden work)
meanwhile
Simona stiffened
into a figure of stone,
her fabricated warmth
under the cold of tears.
She waits for the moss,
the injuries of rain,
vine shoots and birdshit.
She'll decay to be warmed
to a life that we want to share,
patience!

—*Translated from the German by David Young*

(from *Anlässe und Steingärten, 1966*)

Gunnar Ekelöf [Sweden]
1907–1968

Born of a well-to-do Swedish family, Gunnar Ekelöf grew up feeling himself to be an outsider, in part because of his father's mental illness. As a young adult, he studied in London, Uppsala, and Paris, concentrating in music and Oriental culture. Upon returning from Paris, he published his first collection, *Sent på jorden* (Late on the Earth) in 1932, a work influenced by Parisian culture, most particularly Stravinsky's music. Today that work is considered the first truly modernist work of Swedish poetry, and is recognized internationally.

The following volumes were infused with Ekelöf's love of music, his own deep attraction to and speculation on death, and his interest in the nature of man. *Non serviam* of 1945 is one of the most significant of the works of these years, comparing the intellectual world with the metaphysical. And over the next decades, he continued to draw on these sources for poetry: *Om hösten* (In Fall) (1951), *Strountes* (Rubbish) (1955), and *Opus incertum* (Uncertain Work) (1959). He also wrote a long autobiographical poem *En Mölna-elegi* (1960).

In 1958, after having won most Scandinavian literary prizes, Ekelöf became a member of the Swedish Royal Academy.

BOOKS OF POETRY:

Sent på jorden (Stockholm: Spekstrum, 1932); *Dedikation* (Stockholm: Albert Bonniers Förlag, 1934); *Sorgen och stjärnan* (Stockholm: Albert Bonniers Förlag, 1936); *Köp den blindes sång* (Stockholm: Albert Bonniers Förlag, 1938); *Färjesång* (Stockholm: Albert Bonniers Förlag, 1941); *Non serviam* (Stockholm: Albert Bonniers Förlag, 1945); *Om hösten* (Stockholm: Albert Bonniers Förlag, 1951); *Strountes* (Stockholm: Albert Bonniers Förlag, 1955); *Dikter 1932–1951* (Stockholm: Albert Bonniers Förlag, 1956); *Opus incertum* (Stockholm: Albert Bonniers Förlag, 1959); *En Mölna-elegi* (Stockholm: Albert Bonniers Förlag, 1960); *En natt i Otocac* (Stockholm: Albert Bonniers Förlag, 1961); *Sent på jorden, med Appendix 1962, och En Natt Vid Horisonten* (Stockholm: Albert Bonniers Förlag, 1962); *Diwan över Fursten av Emgión* (Stockholm: Albert Bonniers Förlag, 1965); *Dikter* (Stockholm: Albert Bonniers Förlag, 1965); *Sagan om Fatumeh* (Stockholm: Albert Bonniers Förlag, 1966); *Vägvisare till underjorden* (Stockholm: Albert Bonniers Förlag, 1967); *Urval: Dikter 1928–1968* (Stockholm: Albert Bonniers Förlag, 1968); *Partitur* (Stockholm: Albert Bonniers Förlag, 1969); *Lägga patience* (1969); *En självbiografi* (prose and poetry) (Stockholm: Albert Bonniers Förlag, 1971); *En röst* (Stockholm: Albert Bonniers Förlag, 1973); *Dikter 1965–1968* (Stockholm: Albert Bonniers Förlag: 1976); *Variationer* (Lund: Ellerströms, 1986).

ENGLISH LANGUAGE TRANSLATIONS:

Late Arrival on Earth, trans. by Robert Bly and Christina Paulston (London: Rapp & Carroll, 1967); *I Do Best Alone at Night*, trans. by Robery Bly and Christina Paulston (Washington: D.C.:

The Charioteer Press, 1968); *Selected Poems of Gunnar Ekelöf*, trans. by Muriel Rukeyser and Leif Sjöberg (New York: Twayne Publishers, 1967); *Selected Poems by Gunnar Ekelöf*, trans. by W.H. Auden and Leif Sjöberg (New York: Pantheon Books, 1971); reprinted as *Gunnar Ekelöf: Selected Poems* (Harmondsworth, England: Penguin Books, 1971); *A Mölna Elegy*, trans. by Muriel Rukeseyser and Leif Sjöberg (Cambridge, England: Cambridge University Press, 1979; Greensboro, N.C.: Unicorn Press, 1984); *Guide to the Underworld*, trans. by Rika Lesser (Amherst: University of Massachusetts Press, 1980); *Songs of Something Else*, trans. by Leonard Nathan and James Larson (Princeton, New Jersey: Princeton University Press, 1982); *Friends, You Drank Some Darkness: Martinson, Ekelöf, and Tranströmer. Selected Poetry*, trans. by Robert Bly (Boston: Beacon Press, 1984).

Sonata Form Denatured Prose

crush the alphabet between your teeth yawn vowels, the fire is burning in hell vomit
and spit now or never I and dizziness you or never dizziness now or never.
  we will begin over
  crush the alphabet macadam and your teeth yawn vowels, the sweat runs in hell I
am dying in the convolutions of my brain vomit now or never dizziness I and you. i
and he she it. we will begin over. i and he she and it. we will begin over. i and he she it.
we will begin over. i and he she it. scream and cry: it goes fast what tremendous speed
in the sky and hell in my convolutions like madness in the sky dizziness. scream and
cry: he is falling he has fallen. it was fine it went fast what tremendous speed in the sky
and hell in my convolutions vomit now or never dizziness i and you. i and he she it. we
will begin over. i and he she it. we will begin over. i and he she it. we will begin over. i
and he she it.
  we will begin over.
  crush the alphabet between your teeth yawn vowels the fire is burning in hell vomit
and split now or never i and dizziness you or never dizziness now or never.

  —*Translated from the Swedish by Robert Bly and Christina Paulston*

(from *Sent på jorden*, 1932)

To Remember

1
On the bridge

Flowering apple under cleared sky,
leafing birches against the evening,
green and rain fresh....
And there, like an ark
in the meadow sea of mist,
the barn floating
a clouded red....

Voices near
and voices in the distance—
the sadness of spring twilight...
We used to stand on the bridge.
We stood there a long time
in the deepening blue nights
when the pike leaped

—saw the rings spread,
saw the moon path become
a winding serpent
in last year's reeds....
The boys' bikes against the rails....
The echo from farms, distant laughter,
a wave of lilac fragrance
quiet conversation
spring night.

2

With a stake for a mast
and an old sheet for a sail
I tacked the river
which the spring flood had broadened to a lake.
The soggy fields lay under water.
Menyanthes blossoming like falling snow
shone as flakes shine
just before the crystals fade.

But day after day the reeds
built their green wall always higher
around the winding furrow,
and barring the road, concealed it....

Then came the windless high summer days
with air trembling over parched trails
and muttering thunder far off.
The great ashes listened wearily
and in the courtyard the dog half slept.
Through the open window,
whose blind moved itself slowly,
you heard the chugging of the pump,
drowsy clatter of the digging machines
and distant tinkling of tiles
inswept in the wild vine's choir of insects
as in a humming dream.

—*Translated from the Swedish by Leonard Nathan
and James Larson*

(from *Köp den blindes sång*, 1938)

Sketch from the steppes

Grass horizons—
no time, no space
but eternal space
and in the dusk the earthly
tones of a willow pipe....

How holy the thoughts ascend
in this open landscape!
Nothing to stop at,
only the tents that move and move
and beyond the horizon
new horizons....

Grass and space,
horse and soul,
life and death
and a human grip.

*—Translated from the Swedish by Leonard Nathan
and James Larson*

(from *Köp den blindes sång*, 1938)

Absentia animi

In the fall
In the fall when you say goodbye
In the fall when all gates stand open
        toward meaningless pastures
where unreal mushrooms rot
and watery wheel ruts run on their way
to nothing, and a snail is on its way
a tattered butterfly is on its way
to nothing, which is a bloomed-out rose
the smallest and homeliest. And the daddy-long-legs,
        those idiotic devils
delicate-limbed, drunken in the evening lamplight
and the lamp itself softly hums
in the light's negative sea, thought's polar sea
in long waves

silently frothing foam
of series divided by series
from nothing through nothing to nothing
thesis antithesis synthesis abrasax abraxas Thesis
(like the sound of a sewing machine)
And the spiders spin their webs in the quiet night
and crickets chirr
          Meaningless.
Unreal. Meaningless.
                    In the fall

It rustles in my poem
Words do their duty and lie there
Dust falls over them, dust or dew
till the wind swings up and drops (them) down
          (and) elsewhere
he who *partout* seeks the meaning of everything
          long ago found
that the meaning of rustling is rustling
which in itself is something quite distinct from
wet rubber boots in leaves
distracted footsteps through the carpet of the park
of leaves, affectionately sticking
on wet rubber boots, absent-minded steps
You are wandering off, losing yourself
Don't be in such a rush
Stop a little
Wait
In the fall when
In the fall when all gates
then it happens that in the last slanted ray
                    after a day's rain
              with long pauses hestitating
                    as if caught in the act
a left-over thrush sings in a tree top
for nothing, for the sake of his throat. You see
his tree top rise against the pale *fond* of the sky
beside a solitary cloud. And the cloud floats
like other clouds but also left over, *hors saison*
and its very essence long since elsewhere
and in itself (like the song) already something
                    other than

Eternal rest
Meaningless. Unreal.
　　　Meaningless. I
sing sit here
about the sky about a cloud
I wish nothing more for myself
I wish myself a long way off
I am far off (among the echoes of evening)
I am here
Thesis antithesis abrasax
You also I
O far far away
there swims in the bright sky
a cloud over the crown of a tree
in happy unawareness!
O deep down in me
from the surface of the eye of black pearl
is reflected in happy half-awareness
a picture of a cloud!
It is not this that is
It is something else
It exists in what is
but is not this that is
It is something else
O far far away
in what is distant
there is something close!
O deep down in me
in what is near
there is something distant
something remotely near
in what is here yet remote
something neither nor
in what is either or:
neither cloud nor picture
neither picture nor picture
neither cloud nor cloud
neither neither nor nor
but something else!
The only thing that is
is something else!
The only thing that is
in what is

is something else!
The only thing that is
in this that is
is what in this
is something else!
(O lullaby of the soul
the song of something else!)

O
non sens
non sentiens non
dissentiens
indesinenter
terque quaterque
pluries
vox
vel abracadabra

Abraxas abrasax
Thesis, antithesis, synthesis which becomes thesis again
      Meaningless.
Unreal. Meaningless

And the spiders spin their webs in the quiet night
and the crickets chirr
      In the fall

    —*Translated from the Swedish by Leonard Nathan and James Larson*

(from *Non serviam*, 1945)

Elegy

I turned away and everything was changed
The spring thrust out its bird's view eye
From the misty sun straight lines ran to all things
Over the monotonous spans of the telephone wires
    clouds loomed like a fire at sea....
Waves
Waves my sisters for whom do you weep
the young god of evening or the shepherd of pain
I write distracted by thought, perhaps I don't remember it
    any more

but I believe he was blind
What did he whisper in his sleep under the white membrane
Who really knows, but it seemed to make an impression on nature
Great tears hung in the trees
and the clouds lolled weeping along the horizons
I write distracted by thought, perhaps I don't remember it any more
but I believe that he was dead
What was it he saw under the dark membrane
Who knows, who knows, but the stones turned themselves in sleep
A temblor shook all the mountains and the sun turned away
and the sea became bitter
It happened long ago
I don't really know what happened
I remember it only in my feelings
Perhaps it was something else
Perhaps it could have been said in other words
as always everywhere and nowhere
Waves
Waves which hide his traces or hers
all that is written in water and sand

—*Translated from the Swedish by Leonard Nathan and James Larson*

(from *Om Hösten*, 1951)

Greece

O whitewashed chapel
with icons worn out by kisses!
Your door is shut
only with a spike and a twist of wool
such as one gathers among thistles
and twines around the finger
The oil cruse stands ready
and the greasy lamp, and the plate
for him who has a penny
for him who has matches
Old and new icons
a gift of mothers
—occasions have not been wanting—
for him who was left in the pass
for him who was taken as a janissary

for him whose eyesight was emptied
for him who was lost with Markos—
cheap prints under glass
Big as a sheepcote:
Your bells the sheepbells
tinkling somewhere up in the mountains
chapel whose lock is wool.

*—Translated from the Swedish by Leonard Nathan
and James Larson*

(from *Opus incertum*, 1959)

PERMISSIONS

"Sonata Form Denatured Prose"
Reprinted from *Friends, You Drank Some Darkness: Martinson, Ekelöf, and Tranströmer. Selected Poetry,*
trans. by Robert Bly (Boston: Beacon Press, 1984). Reprinted by permission of Robert Bly.

"To Remember," "Sketch from the Steppes," "Absentia animi," "Elegy," and "Greece,"
Reprinted from *Songs of Something Else,* trans. by Leonard Nathan and James Larson (Princeton, New Jersey: Princeton University Press, 1982). Copyright ©1982 by Princeton University Press. Reprinted by permission of Princeton University Press.

J.[osep] [Arseni] V.[icenç] Foix [Spain/writes in Catalan] 1893–1987

Born in Barcelona in 1893, Foix grew up the son of a businessman who ran two bakery shops. He attended grade school in Sarrià and high school at the Colegi Ibéric in Barcelona. At the University of Barcelona, he studied law, but dropped out to help with the family business and—keeping it from his conservative parents—to write.

His early influences included the major Catalonian poets, Mossèn Jacint Verdaguer, Joan Maragall, and Miguel Costa i Llobera, as well as the contemporay French and Spanish-language poets such as Rubén Dario, Charles Riba, and Gabriel Ferrater. And the influence of these poets is revealed in his early works of the 1930s such as *Gertrudis*, KRTU, and *Sol, i de dol*.

But already this early work was closely involved with visual images, and by the time of his publication of *Les Irreals Omegues* in 1949 Foix reveals the influences of modernism shared by his artist friends Joan Miró and Salvador Dalí, as well as his colleague Josep Junoy, with whom he experimented with visual poetry, and his poet friend Paul Eluard. And throughout his long career, Foix would combine surrealist-like images and radical visual and lingusitic experimentations. Despite his attraction to the avant-garde, however, Foix preferred to be free of labels, describing hismself as an "investigator in poetry."

Foix continued to write up until the time of his death, assuring his centrality in the tradition of Catalan literature throughout the century.

BOOKS OF POETRY:

Gertrudis (Barcelona: L'Amic de les Arts, 1927); KRTU (Barcelona: L'Amic de les Arts, 1932); *Sol, i de dol* (Barcelona: L'Amic de les Arts, 1936); *Les Irreals Omegues* (Barcelona: L'Amic de les Arts, 1949); *Còpia d'una lletra tramesa a na Madrona Puignau, de Palau Ça Verdera* (Barcelona: Dau al Set, 1951); *On He Deixat les Claus...* (Barcelona: L'Amic de les Arts, 1953); *Del "Diari 1918"* (Barcelona: Horta, 1956); *Onze Nadals i un Cap d'Any* (Barcelona: L'Amic de les Arts, 1960); *Antología lírica*, edited by Enrique Badosa (Madrid: Rialp, 1963); *L'Estrella d'en Perris* (Barcelona: Fontanella, 1963); *Obres poètiques de J. V. Foix* (Barcelona: Nauta, 1964); *Escenificació de cinc poemes* (Barcelona: Rocas, 1965); *Els lloms transparents* (Barcelona: Edicions 62, 1969); *Antología de J. V. Foix* (bilingual edition in Catalan and Castilian), edited by Enrique Badosa (Barcelona: Plaza & Janés, 1969); *Darrer comunicat* (Barcelona: Edicions 62, 1970); *Allò que no diu La Vanguardia* (Barcelona: Proa, 1970); *Mots i maons; o, A cascú el seu* (Barcelona: L'Amic de les Arts, 1971); *Tocant a mà* (Barcelona: Edicions 62, 1972); *Desa aquests llibres al calaix de baix* (Barcelona: Natua, 1972); *Antología poètica* (Barcelona: Proa, 1973); *Obres completes*, 3 volumes (Barcelona: Edicions 62, 1974, 1979, 1985); *Una Lleu sorra* (Barcelona: Edicions 62, 1975); *Set sonets* (Barcelona: Ferrer, 1984); *Poemes i dibuixos* (Barcelona: Taller de Picasso, 1984); XL *sonets*

(Barcelona: Asociacion de Bibliofilos de Barcelona, 1986); *Album Foix* (Barcelona: Quaderns Crema, 1990).

ENGLISH LANGUAGE TRANSLATIONS:

As for Love, trans. by M.L. Rosenthal (New York: Oxford University Press, 1987); *When I Sleep, Then I See Clearly*, trans. by David H. Rosenthal (New York: Persea, 1988)

Bring on the Oars...

Bring on the oars, my family's always been wanderers,
The sun hangs on my chest amid coral beads
And I say, on board, that I long for peaks and valleys,
For cows milked in a barn while snow falls outside.

Wolves have never scared me; at home
I chase warlocks by torchlight
And, covered with sacks, I sleep beside horses
Or knead, with dead arms, unleavenable bread.

It is I who trod the young vine and stared at that old lady,
And I dive into cold gorges if the lad splits asunder
Or embrace the moon in its difficult meanderings.

One must take risks on land and sea, and in new art,
Kiss a soaked body beneath cinnamon trees
And drop dead at thirty-threee, just like Alexander!

—Translated from the Catalan by David H. Rosenthal

When I spied my rival in the distance, motionlessly awaiting me on the beach, I wondered if it was him, my horse, or Gertrude. As I approached, I realized it was a stone phallus, gigantic, erected in the far-off past. Its shadow covered half the sea and an indecipherable legend was inscribed at the base. I went closer so I could copy it, but before me, lying open on the burning sand, was only my umbrella. Upon the sea, without shadow of ships or clouds, floated those enormous gloves worn by the mysterious monster who chased you toward evening beneath the Ribera's plane trees.

—Translated from the Catalan by David H. Rosenthal

Practice

It's absurd: they said I had to address you, and that at the very hour when sun, sea, and flesh weave dense arborescences and our ghosts wander through this miraculous jungle, I had to deliver a monologue without noticing that there were just a few dozen mummies before me, tragically sentenced to withstand the termite forever. You are by no means unknown to me. I've seen you in funeral processions at the parish storm door and within your moldy chambers, lying on mysterious slipcovered sofas. But I can imitate your faces, if need be, and like yours, my tight-stretched skin is a mask that allows me to behave with the idiocy of one who speaks because his fellow listens. It's absurd, it's absurd. No matter what I might uselessly seek to tell you, a flash of eyes across the sky makes it intelligible to our joyous shadow, which it guides through the jungle our carnal figurations have deserted. My pedantry, then, will humbly recite another's texts. In the jagged blanks between paragraph and paragraph, between author and author, o sister mummies, perhaps you will find those footprints revealing which way my Philips went.

1

An outside spool unwinds thousands and thousands of yards of black gauze before my eyes. That portrait on the wall I'll never get to hang straight again: Is it Blake? Is it Lenin? Is it my father at thirty-five?

2

After passing through a dense forest of deflated tires, I finally got to touch his shoulder. He has glass eyes and a curly beard like the one on that giant at Poldo's house in Solsona.

3

A sofa on a riverbank is truly a marvel. A man bowed beneath the weight of a huge R slowly advances. He places the initial on the sofa, which teeters and falls into the river. But the river's made of glass and splits in a jagged crack from one bank to the other. If I lie down to touch it and see how thick it is, my hand will start bleeding. A voice makes the poplars tremble deep inside like theater props, and it calls out: MARTA! I simultaneously repeat the name (Could I be the only one who shouted it?): That R must have been an M; it *is* an M; no, it's an R. If only the man who brought it would return! But he's ashamed to be seen in shirtsleeves now that the curtain's risen.

4

If it weren't in such bad shape, we'd take the Ford out of its corner and go for a spin. But it doesn't have wheels! Nevertheless, Ernest Maragall hangs a clay angel above the radiator, clutching a piece of paper in its oustretched hands: *Gloria in excelsis Deo.* That's no Ford, it's a Mathis 717171. If it runs smoothly we'll go pick up Feliça (?), Maria Pepa and Niup (?). There's a dance at the Sant Gervasi Atheneum. But we're all naked and Maragall, jerking my head as though he wanted to strangle me, keeps repeating: "I never wear sport jackets! I never wear sport jackets!"

5

"It's not a horse. Among the grapevines, you say? But with a sea this hairy, the moon's whinnies are only audible at midnight, beneath Garraf's tunnels."

6

The coconut-vendor put on a false mustache so big it made me weep with fear. He took my hand and led me to the back of the stable where the horses slept. To keep me quiet, he showed me, through a cobwebbed crack, the vague landscape where a thousand silver rivers die in the sea,and he filled my hands with olives.

—Translated from the Catalan by David H. Rosenthal

With Cold-Numbed Body, I Opened Drawers
Where I Kept Thousands of Poems I Couldn't Remember Writing.
Pilar Assured Me—The Leafy Evening's Low Sky Sparkled with Lips—
That She Had Read Them. The Drawers Were Full of Hard,
Compact Hands That Clutched Mine with Strange Intentions

In what dark sea did a schooner sink
With birds deliriously wheeling above spars
And swooning sails that came to rest beneath moss

    —We pulled the petals from lilacs amid ashes.

In what blind grotto are there seashells
Where we hide treasures of roots and water
Eager for the dance, arming ourselves with reeds

    —Outside town we trod upon shadows.

In what unknown courtyard in a sealed home
Did we hear chants of celestial anguish,
Winged insects upon warm outstretched palms

    —Halfway down the gorge we doused our lanterns.

In the back of what tavern beyond the centuries
Did we taste new wines as we sat bewitched
By the sounds of archaic marble in fossil organs

    —We frightened each other with spectral masks.

In what ancient ravine, vital, did we dance
To the nocturnal plaints of swaying groves,
Lunar echo of voices and sea-chanteys

 —We hid our bodies beneath nets.

On what street did we hear rustling algae
When silent, we bade each other farewell,
Bathed in the light of sparkling predictions

 —Wearing new gloves, we scrutinized pearls.

In what hangar on ancient flatlands
In evening dress and crowned with roses
Did we stroke birds' feathers with trembling hands

 —We started hopeless engines.

At what fountain in lost shadow
One naked summer in open night
Were vestals weeping before gods of stone

 —Blindfolded eyes sang of misfortunes.

Above what wall in an hourless night
Did we write names we couldn't understand
And sketch, shame-facedly, lines that were dead

 —With mouths intact, we dulled lustrous lacquers.

At what turning of pale pathway
Did the girls fall from their bicycles,
Plummeting over the cliffs bright and airy

 —We crossed ourselves with divining water.

In what fathomless drawers did I seek
Poems never written, that I recall
On crumpled paper and in forged handwriting

 —I packed away china and ivory hands.

Cadaqués, September 1930

 —*Translated from the Catalan by David H. Rosenthal*

We Would Have Split More Pines
if the Oxen Hadn't Stared at Us So Fixedly

Hoist our anchors and gaze at the vaulting sky!
Butterflies sprout from your eyes
And altars branch from hermitage ceilings;
With palm leaves I imitate the beaks of birds.
Waters spray and reeds moan,
Ships hug the shore in the inlet's compass.

(This isn't the path;
                    nor the next one;
                                        there's a pool ahead.)

Hearts thirstily float upon gusty fields of grain.

(It's on the other side, where you'll see a footbridge.)

Blue petals sail upon an ocean of lifting fog,
The oxen's calm pupils mirror deep antediluvian seas,
Raised axes paint warlike symbols amid thick smoke
        shadowing bushes.

Solar poplars fan black windows.

Tell me who you are.
  "I don't know where I am."
    Tell me what you're doing.
        "I don't know where I'm from."

Let's plunge dark carving knives into polyhedrons of lard.

August 1931

—Translated from the Catalan by David H. Rosenthal

Beyond the Centuries, Immobile

Walls of lime, inaccessible,
The insistent sea, inexorable turquoise
Filling the docile beach with day and night,
With setting suns and tree-trimmed moons;

And you, and I, immobile through the centuries
At the shadowy foot of an eternal column.
We no longer gaze at each other with fiery pupils,
Nor do we, absent, peer into others' eyes
—Permanent transients
Amid white adverse walls
And the nets that conceal abysses behind doors—.
They bear in their hands the most useless of tools,
And pass by, and return,
And strew black feathers upon the sand.
The aroma of fresh-baked bread drifts through caverns,
Our bodies' pink marble,
Far-off latent snow-capped peaks,
Tar's high-billowing fragrant smoke,
And sleepwalkers, present in their timeless passing,
Are the breath of all:
A school of fish bursts into sparks,
Then thrashes in the hollow left by receding waves
Or echoless pulsing in the One Supreme Beat,
Tossing our nets from the tip of the Cape.

El Port de la Selva, August 1931

—Translated from the Catalan by David H. Rosenthal

PERMISSIONS

"Bring on the Oars…," "[When I spied my rival]," "Practice," "With Cold-Numbered Body, I Opened Drawers…," "We Would Have Split More Pines if the Oxen Hadn't Stared At Us So Fixedly," "Beyond the Centuries, Immobile"
Reprinted from *When I Sleep, Then I See Clearly*, trans. by David H. Rosenthal (New York: Persea, 1988). Copyright ©1985 by J. V. Foix. English language copyright ©1988 by David Rosenthal. Reprinted by permission of Persea Books, Inc.

Ángel González [Spain]
1925

Born in 1925 in Oviedo, Spain, Ángel González lived his early youth in northern Spain. His father died two years after his birth, and he was brought up by his mother in the period of the Spanish Civil War. One brother was killed during the conflict, and another was left home to fight on the side of the Republicans. Both his mother and sister lost their jobs, and the family lived in extreme poverty.

In his early years González displayed a great interest in music, and might have gone on to study it if it were not for their poverty. He was, however, able to attend the University of Oviedo, where he studied law, graduating in 1948. During this same period he had begun to write poetry, particularly during a period when he contracted tuberculosis and was sent to a small town in the mountains of Léon. Thereafter, he took a job as music critic for the periodical *La voz de Asturias* in Oviedo. In 1951 he traveled to Madrid to take a course at the Official School of Journalism. But with the extreme propaganda of the time, he decided to abandon journalism and entered into government service in the Ministry of Public Works, first in Seville and later in Madrid, a job he was to retain until the early 1970s.

In Madrid, González became a regular in the informal meetings of writers and other intellectuals at the Café Pelayo and in Barcelona. It was there he became acquainted with other Spanish poets, such as Jaime Gil de Biedma, Gabriel Celaya, Vicente Aleixandre, Carlos Barral, and Juan García Hortelano. Although he, himself, had largely abandoned his early poetic efforts, Aleixandre and others encouraged him to continue writing.

In 1956 he published *Aspero mundo*, which contained poems mostly written before his move to Madrid. It was nominated for one of the major literary prizes (the Adonáis Prize), and the response to the book further encouraged him to continue writing. A trip to France, Italy, Scandinavia, West Germany, and Czechoslovakia in 1957 further provided González with new sources and literary contacts. In 1961 he published his second book, *Sin esperanza, con convencimiento* (Without Hope, but with Conviction). His third volume, even more social in its message, was *Grado elemental* (Elementary Grade) (1962), a book which assured González's place as one of the major figures of the "Generation of 1950."

During the early 1970s González traveled to the Universidad Nacional Autóonoma de México, and from there accepted a position of visiting professor at the University of New Mexico in the United States. White teaching he New Mexico, he met Shirley Mangini, a graduate student, whom he married. Over the next few years, González accepted similar one-year appointments at various American universities, including the University of Utah, the University of Maryland, and the University of Texas. He assumed a permanent position as professor of contemporary Spanish literature at the University of New Mexico in 1975.

BOOKS OF POETRY:

Aspero mundo (Madrid: Rialp, 1956); *Sin esperanza, con convencimiento* (Barcelona: Literaturasa, 1961); *Grado elemental* (Paris: Ruedo Ibérico, 1962); *Palabra sobre palabra* (Madrid: Poesía para Todos, 1965; revised and enlarged editions (Barcelona: Seix Barral, 1968, 1972, 1977); *Tratado de urbanismo* (Barcelona: Bardo, 1967); *Breves acotaciones para una biografía* (Las Palmas, Grand Canary Island: Inventarios Provisionales, 1971); *Muestra de algunos procedimientos narrativos y de las actitudes sentimentales que habitualmente comportan* (Madrid: Turner, 1976; revised and enlarged 1977); *Poemas* (Madrid: Cátedra, 1980); *Antología poética* (Madrid: Alianza, 1982).

ENGLISH LANGUAGE TRANSLATIONS:

Harsh World and Other Poems, trans. by Donald D. Walsh (Princeton: Princeton University Press, 1977); *Astonishing World: The Selected Poems of Ángel González 1958–1986*, trans. by Steven Ford Brown and Gutierrez Revuelta (Minneapolis: Milkweed Editions, 1993).

Before I Could Call Myself Ángel González

Before I could call myself Ángel González,
before the earth could support the weight of my body,
a long time
and a great space were necessary:
men from all the seas and all the lands,
fertile wombs of women, and bodies
and more bodies, incessantly fusing
into another new body.
Solstices and equinoxes illuminated
with their changing lights, and variegated skies,
the millenary trip of my flesh
as it climbed over centuries and bones.
Of its slow and painful journey,
of its escape to the end, surviving
shipwrecks, anchoring itself
to the last sigh of the dead,
I am only the result, the fruit,
what's left, rotting, among the remains;
what you see here,
is just that:
tenacious trash resisting
its ruin, fighting against wind,
walking streets that go
nowhere. The success
of all failures. The insane
force of dismay...

—*Translated from the Spanish by Steven Ford Brown
and Gutierrez Revuelta*

(from *Palabra sobre palabra*, 1964)

Dogs Against the Moon

Dogs against the moon, very far away,
bring closer
the restlessness of the murmuring
night. Clear
sounds, once inaudible,
are now heard. Vague echoes,

shreds of words, creaking
hinges,
disturb the shadowed circle.

Scarcely without space,
the silence, the silence
you can't hold, closed in
by sounds, presses
against your arms and legs,
rises gently to your head,
and falls through your loosened hair.

It's night and the dream: don't be uneasy.
The silence has grown like a tree.

       —Translated from the Spanish by Steven Ford Brown
         and Gutierrez Revuelta

(from *Palabra sobre palabra*, 1964)

Astonishing World

An astonishing world
suddenly looms up.

I'm afraid of the moon
embalmed
in the waters of the river,
the silent forest
that scratches with its branches
the belly of the rain,
birds
that howl in the tunnel of night
and everything
that unexpectedly
makes a gesture and smiles
only to suddenly disappear.

In the midst
of the cruel retreat of things
rushing in headlong flight toward
nothingness and ashes,

my heart goes under in the shipwreck
of the fate of the world that surrounds it.
Where does the wind go, that light,
the cry
of the unexpected red poppy,
the singing of the gray
sea gulls of the ports?

And what army is it that takes me
wrapped up in its defeat and its flight
—I, a prisoner, a weary hostage,
without name or number, handcuffed
among squads of fugitive cries—
toward the shadows where the lights go,
toward the silence where my voice dies.

> —*Translated from the Spanish by Steven Ford Brown*
> *and Gutierrez Revuelta*

(from *Palabra sobre palabra*, 1964)

Yesterday

Yesterday was Wednesday all morning.
By afternoon it changed:
it became almost Monday,
sadness invaded hearts
and there was a distinct
panic of movement toward
the trolleys
that take the swimmers down to the river.

At about seven a small plane slowly
crossed the sky, but not even the children
watched it.
      The cold
was unleashed,
someone went outdoors wearing a hat,
yesterday, and the whole day
was like that,
already you see,
how amusing,

yesterday and always yesterday and even now,
strangers
are constantly walking through the streets
or happily indoors snacking on
bread and coffee with cream: what
joy!

Night fell suddenly,
the warm yellow street lamps were lit,
and no one could
impede the final dawn
of today's day,
so similar
and yet
so different in lights and aroma!

For that very same reason,
because everything is just as I told you,
let me tell you
about yesterday, once more
about yesterday: the incomparable
day that no one will ever
see again upon the earth.

> —*Translated from the Spanish by Steven Ford Brown
> and Gutierrez Revuelta*

(from *Palabra sobre palabra*, 1964)

The Future

But the future is different
from that destiny seen from afar,
magical world, vast sphere
brushed by the long arm of desire,
brilliant ball the eyes dream,
shared dwelling
of hope and deception, dark
land
of illusion and tears
the stars predicted
and the heart awaits
and that is always, always, always distant.

But, I think, the future is also another thing:
a verb tense in motion, in action, in combat,
a searching movement toward life,
keel of the ship that strikes the water
and struggles to open between the waves
the exact breach the rudder commands.

I'm on this line, in this deep
trajectory of agony and battle,
trapped in a tunnel or trench
that with my hands I open, close, or leave,
obeying the heart that orders,
pushes, determines, demands, and searches.

Future of mine...! Distant heart
that dictated it yesterday:
don't be ashamed.
Today is the result of your blood,
pain that I recognize, light that I admit,
suffering that I assume,
love that I intend.

But still, nothing is definitive.
Tomorrow I have decided to go ahead
and advance,
tomorrow I am prepared to be content,
tomorrow I will love you, morning
and night,
tomorrow will not be exactly as God wishes.

Tomorrow, gray or luminous, or cold,
that hands shape in the wind,
that fists draw in the air.

> —*Translated from the Spanish by Steven Ford Brown
> and Gutierrez Revuelta*

(from *Palabra sobre palabra*, 1964)

Words Taken from a Painting by José Hernández

1.—*The first light of day*

A rooster sings stones:
daybreak.

(Thin, pallid, translucent moon,
immobile, rigid, fused with sky.)

Against the tiles,
against the glass,
a rooster sings blood.

                    (The wind
sifts through the sleeping trees.)

A rooster's song crests,
it sings gall-nuts,
spits its gizzard against the sky.

Green fruits spill down
the slopes into the ravines.

Knocking on doors, windows,
the rooster's insistent song warns you.

(Vultures high on the rocks
stretch their enormous wings.)

A rooster lays a stream of fire
across the white border of night.

Nothing else could happen: shouts, threats.
It's just been announced the truce has ended.

2.—*End of the last act*

At the grand finale
           the opera is finished
part of the platform
           an ovation

collapses
explodes against the wall
tearing the paper decorations
the curtain doesn't fall
a crack
an almost invisible cry
appears, expands
from the last singer
(lizard of ash
hangs for a moment
ant-hill of dust
in the shining
an invading
crystalline
spider
nothingness
that reaches into everything
sliding at last
with its flexible forelegs
through the divided cupola
from the sky's most frightening obscurity
into another more amplified nothingness
frightening obscurity
where it disappears forever.

An unforeseen sadness breaks away from the roof
slightly stains
the costumes, the marble, the flowers, foreheads, shadows.
Already nothing is like before.
No body returns
to their true self.
The eyes
can't recognize what they seek.
The emptiness (that was stone
((stone that was flesh (((flesh
that was a cry ((((cry that
was love, fear, hope?))))))))))
is enlarged, deformed,
explodes into a thousand pieces of emptiness
that strikes the already impassive faces.

Phrases fly from gloomy lips,
echoes of banal dialogues
wander through the deserted lobby
like dry seeds suspended in the air

—Where's the exit?
—Yesterday still lacks so much.
                —Excuse me
But the cold follows.
                —No, it's nothing.

like the smoke asleep in an extinguished bonfire,
that the implacable breeze suddenly releases.

          —Translated from the Spanish by Steven Ford Brown
             and Gutierrez Revuelta

(from *Palabra sobre palabra*, 1964)

PERMISSIONS

"Before I Could Call Myself Ángel González," "Dogs Against the Moon," "Astonishing World," "Yesterday,"
"The Future," and "Words Taken from a Painting by José Hernádez"
Reprinted from *Astonishing World: The Selected Poems of Angel González 1958-1986*, trans. by Steven Ford
Brown and Gutierrez Revuelta (Minneapolis: Milkweed Editions, 1993). Copyright ©1986 by Editorial Seix
Barral and Ángel González. English language translation copyright ©1993 by Steven Ford Brown and Gutierrez
Revuelta. Reprinted by permission of Milkweed Editions.

Jorge Guillén [Spain]
1893–1984

Born in Valladolid, Spain, Jorge Guillén was another major poet in the Spanish Generation of 1927, which included figures such as Federico García Lorca, Pedro Salinos, Rafael Alberti, Luis Cernuda, and Vicente Aleixandre.

Guillén attended elementary school at the Instutite of Valladolid, and studied at the Maison Perreyve of the French Fathers of the Oratory in Fribough before attending the universities of Madrid and Granada. His attendance at the Sorbonne in 1917 led him to several other institutions in Oxford, Seville, and—in exile from the Civil War of Spain— Middlebury College in Vermont, McGill University in Toronto, and Wellesley College in Massachusetts. After 1947 he continued in the United States as visiting professor at Harvard, Princeton, and Yale. In 1972 he was awarded the Miguel de Cervantes Prize, one the most important of Hispanic literary honors. He returned to Spain in 1977 after Franco's death. He died in Málaga in 1984.

It was during his French stay that he began to compose his first and one of his most important collections, *Cántico*. That book, published in Madrid in 1928, was immediately recognized as a masterwork. The critic Joaquín Casalduero described the book as perhaps the most "austere" work of Spanish literature, and one of its most "simple, dedicated to one single theme... The composition of *Cántico* is that of a rose."

For many years Guillén was known in Spain as only the author of *Cántico*, but in the late 1950s he published another masterwork, the three volume poetic trilogy, *Clamor*. 1968 saw the publication of another major work, *Aire nuestro* (Our Air), a work, written in his 80s, about the inevitability of death and his continuing affirmation of life.

BOOKS OF POETRY:

Cántico (Madrid: Revisa de Occidente, 1928; revised and enlarged in 1936, 1945, and 1950); *El encanto de las sirenas* (Mexico City: Panamericana, 1953); *El huerto de Melibea* (Madrid: Insula, 1954); *Lugar de Lázaro* (Málaga: Dardo, 1957); *Clamor, tiempo de historia (Maremagnum, Que van a dar en a mar* and *A la altura de las circunstancias)* (Buenos Aires: Sudamericana, 1957, 1960, 1963); *Viviendo y otros poemas* (Barcelona: Seix Barral, 1958); *Poemas de Castilla* (Santiago, 1960); *Suite italienne* (Milan: All'Insegna del Pesce d'Oro, 1964); *Tréboles* (Santander, Spain: Isla de los Ratones, 1964); *Selección de poemas* (Madrid: Gredos, 1965; enlarged 1970); *Relatos* (Málaga: Guadalhorce, 1966); *Homenaje: Reunión de vidas* (Milan: All'Insegna del Pesce d'Oro, 1967); *Antología*, edited by José Manuel Blecua (Salamanca, Spain: Anaya, 1970); *Obra poética* (Madrid: Alianza, 1970); *Y otros poemas* (Buenos Aires: Muchnik, 1973); *Al margen* (Madrid: Visor, 1974); *Convivencia* (Madrid: Turner, 1975); *Mientras el aire es nuestro*, edited by Philip W. Silver (Madrid: Cátedra, 1978); *Poesía amorosa: 1919-1972*, edited by Anne-Marie Couland (Madrid: Cupsa, 1978);

Serie castellana (Madrid: Caballo Griego para la Poesía, 1978); *Algunos poemas,* edited by Angel Caffarena (Santander, Spain: Institución Cultural de Cantabria, 1981); *Antología del mar* (Málaga: Agora, 1981); *La expresión* (Ferrol, Spain: Sociedad de Cultura Valle-Inclán, 1981); *Aire Nuestro: Final* (Barcelona: Seix Barral, 1981); *Poemas malagueños* (Málaga: Publicaciones de la Diputación Provincial de Málaga, 1983); *Sonetos completos* (Granada: Ubago, 1988).

ENGLISH LANGUAGE TRANSLATIONS:

Cántico: A Selection of Spanish Poems, trans. by Norman Thomas di Giovanni and others (Boston: Little, Brown, 1963; London: Deutsch, 1965); *Affirmation: A Bilingual Anthology, 1919–1966,* trans. by Julian Palley (Norman: University of Oklahoma Press, 1968); *Horses in the Air and Other Poems,* trans. by Cola Franzen (San Francisco: City Lights Books, 1999).

The Hills

Purity, solitude? There. They are grey.
Intact greys not even the idle foot
surprised, supremely light. Greys beside
Nothing, melancholy and beautiful, which
the air shelters like a soul, visible
because so true to its object: waiting
always. To be! And even more remote,
for smoke, for eyes of the most distracted,
a secure Nothingness: the perfect grey
on tender aridness, grey of those hills!

—Translated from the Spanish by Julian Palley

Calm of Gardens

The stars advance among
   storm clouds
toward the final garden.
   Stones, flowers.

What of the human accident?
   Block-like quiet.
The dead are more dead
   every night.

Marbles, fronds all alike:
   green is the order.
Over the cypress, stars:
   more verdure.

The dead go on dying.
   Well they remain
in peace and oblivion
   bereft of their names!

May their weariness enjoy
   shade in accord.
The stars approach among
   storm clouds.

—Translated from the Spanish by Julian Palley

The Names

Dawn. The horizon
opens its lashes,
begins to see. What? Names.
They are on the patina

of things. The rose
is still called
rose, and the memory
of its passing, haste.

Haste to live more, more!
May the instant's acrid
plunge lift us, move
us to unending love! So

swift in reaching its
goal it rushes to impose
later! Watch out, I shall
be! And the roses?

Closed eyelids, final
horizon. And there remains
nothing, at all? No,
there are still the names.

—Translated from the Spanish by Julian Palley

Federico García Lorca

*Dedicated also to the memory of
Miguel Hernández*

II

A murmur crosses the silence
with a continual flowing,
a source like dawn among rocks
glimmers above seafoam.
Does a human gaze hesitate on water?
An illumination becomes sharper

as if it were radiant spirit
and moves now toward song
which says...
      It says: life.
Nothing more.
      An invasion
of evidences presses upon us, uplifts
us, convincing without intoxicating,
carries us to light—air. The clearest,
irrefutable nakedness imposes.
Clarity breaks forth,
clarity that is yet human
with its conquering light
approach of a form,
of a gesture that is language,
a creator's triumph,
and with his angel, his *duende*, his muse,
luminous specters,
he leads into plentitude
the humanness of man.

II

A man knows what the tree does not,
what the sea contemplates indifferently.
Through a casual dazzling light
is suddenly discovered....
        What?
Behind life comes death along—
there's no cure—a rigorous succession.

Behond the chosen one.
Does he freely, gladly instill
the joy of his light?
Now it is he who suffers
beneath the somber ray.
Pain, terror, alarm always on guard.

In the shade of this cruel sun,
in spite of the leaden
peace of siestas,
whitewashed walls are a sign,
among cactus and olives,

of an outrage, a crime.
Baleful imminences
will violently
precipitate
the flowing of blood toward a knife
of vengeance, of rage.
Observe him well. He knows best
that final crimson outpour.

III

The countryside surrendered to its blackness,
the sky's deserts without their lights,
the vilest forces prevail
and extend that chaos
not ready for being.
Chaos: a single ocean
of vomit. Hatreds
seek reasons, find madness.
The dead wander lost in silence,
silence among shots.
Sepulchers without headstones.

Will the finest fall?

Something glistens momentarily
and the divination does not err:
The best. Shall fall.

He will not.
          No!
            No!
Eyes are there to see. Has fallen.

The world does not recover soon
from its long stupor.
Despair, tearless,
does not weep.
But the invisble starry cumulus
latently accompanies.

Scattered, distant hearts
join their rage.
Who escapes that universal sorrow?
There are not enough tears
for all the fallen,
for the buried, the unburied.

Creation is destruction.

Even the most eloquent is silenced.
Immortal in us, but dead.
There is no melancholy wind among the olive trees.
Only a despairing wind above the dead man.
Despairing man beside the dead.

—*Translated from the Spanish by Julian Palley*

PERMISSIONS

"The Hills," "Calm of Gardens," "The Names," and "Federico García Lorca"
Reprinted from *Affirmation: A Bilingual Anthology, 1919–1966*, translated with Notes by Juilan Palley (Norman: University of Oklahoma Press, 1968). Reprinted by permission of University of Oklahoma Press.

Hagiwara Sakutarō [Japan]
1886–1942

Born into a wealthy family, Sakutarō was able as a young man to devote himself to poetry. Although he did not finish college, he read Western authors, including Poe, Nietzsche, Schopenhauer, and Dostoevsky.

He began by writing poems in the tanka form, drawn to it in 1901 when he read the collection *Midare-gami* (Hair in Disorder) by Yosano Akiko. Writing poems in this form for about ten years, he stopped in 1910. During this same period Sakutarō moved from his native Maebashi to Kumamoto, then to Okayama and, ultimately, Tokyo, failing his classes in Japanese and unable to complete his schooling.

His father's wealth allowed him to remain in Toyko without any definite goals for three years. There he heard concerts and saw stage productions such as one of *A Doll's House*, and adapted Western attitudes. He also learned to play the mandolin and guitar, and upon his return to his home, founded a musicians' club called Condola Western Music Society, of which he was the conductor.

In early 1913 he began corresponding with the poet Muro'o Saisei, whose poems he had read in the journal *Zamuboa*. In May that magazine published some of his own poems, which meant immediate recognition in Tokyo and began to inspire him to write more poetry. That year, the year of the beginning of First World War, Sakutarō emerged as a notable poet, and by 1915 had written a considerable body of work. Suddenly in 1915, he stopped writing poetry, and attempted suicide because of his continued ill-health and drunkenness. A year of silence ensued, but in 1916 he began to write again, and in February 1917 published his first book of poems, *Tsuki ni hoeru* (Howling at the Moon).

Tsuki ni hoeru received immediate acclaim, in part because it represented one of the first successful attempts to fuse colloquial Japanese with complex ideas and what Hagiwara described as "physiological fear," a fear that, lying deep in one's physical existence, continues to exert a fearful force on the individual's spiritual and mental condition.

His second collection, *Aoneko* (Blue Cat) of 1923 is a work of growing despair and melancholy, in which the cat symbolizes the individual at rest, indulging in fantasies. His *Hyōtō* (Iceland) of 1934 represents a further move of the poet away from society, trapped in his anger for his own ostracization. *Nekomachi* (The Cat People) of the following year was a work of prose-poetry.

Hagiwara also wrote aphorisms, fiction, and critical essays, contributing important works to Japanese literary theory, particularly in *Shi no genri* (Principles of Poetry).

He died in Tokyo in 1942.

[*Based on material by Hiroaki Sato*]

BOOKS OF POETRY:

Tsuki ni hoeru (1917); *Aoneko* (1923); *Junjo Shokyoku Shu* (1925); *Hyōtō* (1934); *Nekomachi* (1935); all volumes are collected in *zenshū* (Tokyo: Chikuma Shobō)

ENGLISH LANGAUGE TRANSLATIONS:

Face at the Bottom of the World and Other Poems, trans. by Graeme Wilson (Rutland, Vermont: C. E. Tuttle, 1969); *Howling at the Moon*, trans. by Hiroaki Sato (Tokyo: University of Tokyo Press, 1978) [translation of *Tsuki ni hoeru* and *Aoneko*]; *Rats' Nests: The Collected Poetry of Hagiwara Sakutaro* (selections), trans. by Robert Epp (Stanwood, Washington: Yakusha, 1993);

Bamboo

Something straight growing on the ground,
something sharp, blue, growing on the ground,
piercing the frozen winter,
in morning's empty path where its green leaves glisten,
shedding tears,
shedding the tears,
now repentance over, from above its shoulders,
blurred bamboo roots spreading,
something sharp, blue, growing on the ground.

—Translated from the Japanese by Hiroaki Sato

Bamboo

On the gleaming ground bamboo growing,
blue bamboo growing,
under the ground bamboo roots growing,
roots gradually tapering off,
from root tips cilia growing,
faintly blurred cilia growing,
faintly trembling.

On the hard ground bamboo growing,
from the ground bamboo sharply growing,
straight, blind, bamboo growing,
at each frozen joint gallantly,
under the blue sky bamboo growing,
bamboo, bamboo, bamboo growing

Behold all sins have been inscribed,
yet not all are mine,
verily manifest to me are
only the illusions of blue flames without shadows,
only the ghosts of pathos that fade off over the snow,
ah painful confessions on such a day, what shall I make of them,
all are but the illusions of blue flames.

—Translated from the Japanese by Hiroaki Sato

Dish of Skylarks

The fresh green and fragrant winds of a May morning
make an aristocrat of my life. Under a dripping sky-
blue window, I would like to ply forks of pure silver
with a woman I love. Someday, once in my life, I
would like to steal and eat that love-plate of skylarks,
which gleams in the sky.

—Translated from the Japanese by Hiroaki Sato

Death

From the bottom of the earth I stare at,
a ridiculous hand sticks out,
a leg sticks out,
a neck protrudes,
gentlemen,
this damned thing, what on earth,
what kind of goose is this?
From the bottom of the earth I stare at,
looking foolish,
a hand sticks out,
a leg sticks out,
a neck protrudes.

—Translated from the Japanese by Hiroaki Sato

Frog's Death

A frog was killed,
the children made a circle and raised their hands,
all, together,
raised their lovely,
bloody hands,
the moon appeared,
on the hill stands a man.
Under his hat, a face.

—*Translated from the Japanese by Hiroaki Sato*

The Reason the Person Inside Looks Like a Deformed Invalid

I am standing in the shadow of a *lace* curtain,
that is the reason my face looks vague.
I am holding a telescope in my hands,
I am looking through it far into the distance,
I am looking at the woods,
where dogs and lambs made of nickel and children with bald heads
      are walking,
those are the reasons my eyes look *somewhat* smoked over.
I ate too much of the plate of *cabbage* this morning,
and besides this windowglass is very shoddily made,
that is the reason my face looks so excessively distorted.
To tell you the truth,
I am healthy, perhaps too healthy,
and yet, why are you staring at me, there?
Why smiling so eerie a smile?
Oh, of course, as for the part of my body below the waist,
if you are saying that area isn't *clear*,
that's a somewhat foolish question,
of course, that is, close to this pale window wall,
I am standing inside the house.

—*Translated from the Japanese by Hiroaki Sato*

Chair

The person sleeping under the chair,
is he the children of the person who made the grand house?

—Translated from the Japanese by Hiroaki Sato

Spring Night

Things like littlenecks,
things like quahogs,
things like water-fleas,
these organisms, bodies buried in sand,
out of nowhere,
hands like silk threads innumerably grow,
hands' slender hairs move as the waves do.
A pity, on this lukewarm spring night,
purling the brine flows,
over the organisms water flows,
even the tongues of clams, flickering, looking sad,
as I look around at the distant beach,
along the wet beach path,
a row of invalids, bodies below their waists missing, is walking,
walking unsteadily.
Ah, over the hair of those human beings as well,
passes the spring night haze, all over, deeply,
rolling, rolling in,
this white row of waves is ripples.

—Translated from the Japanese by Hiroaki Sato

The World of Bacteria

Bacteria's legs,
bacteria's mouths,
bacteria's ears,
bacteria's noses,

bacteria are swimming.

Some in a person's womb,
some in a clam's intestines,
some in an onion's spherical core,
some in a landscape's center.

Bacteria are swimming.

Bacteria's hands grow right and left, crosswise,
the tips of their hands branch out like roots,
from there sharp nails grow,
capillaries and such spread *all over.*

Bacteria are swimming.

Where bacteria live their lives,
as if through an invalid's skin,
a vermilion light shines thinly in,
and only that area is faintly visible,
looks truly, truly sorrow-unbearable.

Bacteria are swimming.

—Translated from the Japanese by Hiroaki Sato

Lover of Love

I painted *rouge* on my lips,
and kissed the trunk of a new birch,
even if I were a handsome man,
on my chest are no breasts like *rubber balls,*
from my skin rises no fragrance of fine-*textured* powder,
I am a wizened man of ill-fate,
ah, what a pitiable man,
in today's balmy early summer field,
in a stand of glistening trees,
I slipped on my hands sky-blue gloves,
put around my waist something like a *corset,*
smeared on my nape something like nape-powder,
thus hushed assuming a coquettish *pose,*
as young girls do,
I cocked my head a little,
and kissed the trunk of a new birch,
I painted rosy rouge on my lips,
and clung to a tall tree of snowy white.

—Translated from the Japanese by Hiroaki Sato

You Frog

You frog,
in a growth of blue *pampas grass* and *reed,*
the frog looks swollen white,
in the eveningscape with rain falling fully,
gyo, gyo, gyo, gyo croaks the frog.

Slapping down on the coal-black ground,
tonight the rain and the wind are fierce,
even on a cold leaf of grass,
it sucks a sigh in, the frog,
gyo, gyo, gyo, gyo, croaks the frog.

You frog,
my heart is not far from you,
I held a lantern in my hand,
and was watching the face of the dark garden,
was watching, in a tired state of mind, the grass and tree
    leaves wilting in the rain.

—*Translated from the Japanese by Hiroaki Sato*

Skylark Nest

With the saddest heart in the world I walked down the riverbed of my
    home town.
On the riverbed, starworts, horsetails and such, parsley, shepherd's-purse,
    and even the roots of violets profusely grew.
Behind the low sandmound the Toné river flows. Like a thief, darkly
    helplessly flows.
I was still, crouched on the riverbed.
Before my eyes is a bush of riverbed-mugwort.
A handful, the bush is. Like an emaciated woman's hair the mugwort loosely
    moved in the wind.
I am deep in thought about some unsavory thing. A terrible ominous thought.
And, with an almost deranged sun shining upon my hat, muggy, I'm exhausted,
    perspiring.
Like a parched man panting, yearning for water, I shot out my hand.
As if grasping my own soul I grasped *something.*
Grasped something like bone-dry hair.
Hidden in the riverbed-mugwort, a skylark nest.

Piyo, piyo, piyo, piyo, piyo, piyo, piyo, piyo, in the sky a skylark calls.
I gazed at the pitiful skylark nest.
The nest swelled on my large palm, gently as a softball.
The sensation that fawns, seeks love from those innocently raised, was
    apparently felt in my heart.
I became freakishly lonely and felt pain.
Like a parent bird I craned my neck again and peered into the nest.
Inside the nest, as in a beam of light at evening, it was vague
    and dark.
An incomparably DELICATE pathos, like touching the celia of a feeble
    plant, brushed the peripheries of my nerves like a shadow and was gone.
Illuminated by the scant beam of light in the nest, rat-colored skylark eggs,
    about four of them, gleamed solitary.
I stretched my fingers and picked up one of them.
The lukewarm breathing of a living thing tickled the belly of my thumb.
A confounding sensation like looking at a dying dog, boiled up at the bottom
    of my heart.
Of the lukewarm unpleasantness of the sensation of a man at such a moment
    disasterous crimes are born. A heart afraid of crime is the forerunner
    of a heart that gives birth to a crime.
I looked at the egg held between my fingers gently against the sunlight.
Something faintly red and vague was visible like a clot of blood.
Something like cold juice was felt.
At that moment I felt a raw-smelling liquid oozily flowing between my fingers.
The egg was torn.
A barbarian's fingers had savagely crushed a delicate thing.
On the rat-colored thin eggshell the character к was inscribed, red, and lightly.

An exquisite bird-bud, bird's parent.
A nest made with a lovely beak, a small animal's job for which it did its best,
    a manifestation of a loveable instinct.
Various good-natured, demure thoughts welled up violently in the bottom of my heart.
I tore an egg.
Killed love and joy, did a job full of sorrow and curse.
Did a dark unpleasant deed.
I made a gloomy face and looked at the ground.
On the ground pebbles glittered, glass fragments, and grass roots, everywhere.
Piyo, piyo, piyo, piyo, piyo, piyo, piyo, piyo, in the sky the skylark calls.
There's a raw-smelling odor of spring.
I was again deep in thought about that *unsavory* thing.
That a human being dislikes the odor of a human being's skin.
That a human being feels that a human being's sexual organs are hideous.

That at times a human being looks like a horse.
That a human being betrays a human being's love.
That a human being dislikes a human being.
Ah, misanthrope-invalid.
Reading a certain famous Russian's novel, a very heavy novel, I came upon
    the story of a misanthrope-invalid.
It's an excellent novel, but a terrifying novel.
Not to be able to love with one's body those whom one's heart loves, what
    a hideous thought. What a hideous illness.
Not once since I was born have I kissed girls.
Nor have I ever simply put my hand around the shoulders of the birds I love
    and talked like an elder brother.
Ah, birds whom I love, I love, I love.
I love human beings. Nevertheless I fear human beings.
Sometimes I escape from everyone and become solitary. And my heart loving every-
one becomes tearful.
I always like, while walking on a deserted lonely beach, to think of the crowds
    in the distant city.
About the lamp-lighting time in the distant city, I like to walk alone in the park grounds
    of my home town.
Ah, yesterday as usual, I kept dreaming sad dreams.
I smelled the odor of rotten human blood.
I feel pain.
I become lonely.
Why can't one love with one's body those whom one loves with one's heart?
I repent.
Repent.
Whenever I feel pain, I repent.
Sit on the riverbed sand of the Toné river, and repent.

Piyo, piyo, piyo, piyo, piyo, piyo, piyo, piyo, in the sky the skylarks call.
Riverbed-mugwort roots profusely spread.
The Toné river is flowing stealthily like a thief.
Here and there, I see farmers' melancholy faces.
The faces are dark, looking only at the ground.
On the ground, spring, like smallpox, is ponderously erupting.

With what pity I picked up the skylark egg.

—Translated from the Japanese by Hiroaki Sato

Secret of the Garden of a Vacant House Seen in a Dream

Things planted in the garden of the vacant house are pine trees and such
loquat trees, peach trees, black pine trees, sasanquas, cherries, and such
prosperous tree foliage, brances of foliage that spread around
as well, the plants that luxuriate continually under the swarming branches of leafage
all of them—ferns, bracken, fiddleheads, sundews, and such
all over the ground they pile up and crawl
the life of these blue things
the prosperous lives of these blue things
the garden of the vacant house is always in the plants' shadows and dusky
only, what faintly flows is a string of rivulet water
the sound of running water, soughing sad and low, day and night
as well, somewhere near the soggy hedge
I see the uncanny muculent forms of slugs, snakes, frogs, lizards, and such
And above this secluded world
pale moonlight illuminates the night
moonlight flows in mostly through the planted groves.
Heart intent on thoughts of this late night deepening, ever so sad and gentle,
my heart, leaning on the fence, madly plays the flute;
ah, this secret life where various things are hidden
a world where boundlessly beautiful shadows and mysterious forms pile up
focused in moonlight; ferns, bracken, branches of pine trees
the eerie lives of slugs, snakes, lizards, and such
ah, how I miss the secret of the garden of this vacant house I dream of where
    no one lives
and its deeply suggestive seclusion, its mystery ever unsolved.

—Translated from the Japanese by Hiroaki Sato

PERMISSIONS

"Bamboo," "Bamboo," "Dish of Skylarks," "Death," "Frog's Death," "The Reason the Person Inside Looks Like a Deformed Invalid," "Chair," "Spring Night," "The World of Bacteria," "Love of Love," "You Frog," "Skylark Nest," and "Secret of the Garden of a Vacant House Seen in a Dream"
Reprinted from *Howling at the Moon*, trans. by Hiroaki Sato (Tokyo: University of Tokyo Press, 1978). Copyright ©1978 by Hiroaki Sato. Reprinted by permission of Hiroaki Sato and Green Integer.

Hayashi Fumiko [Japan]
1903–1951

Born in Moji in the extreme west of Japan, Hayashi
Fumiko was unacknowledged upon her birth by her
father, thus leaving her and her mother in the posi-
tion of being outcasts. Without the father's registra-
tion, she was left to her mother's registry, a position
in Japan that ostracizes individuals from social ac-
ceptance or family inheritance.

She spent most of her early years as an itinerant
peddler. As her father developed his business, more-
over, he brought home a geisha to live in the house.
Fumiko's mother left with her child and the father's
chief clerk, whose lack of business sense further con-
tributed to their destitute condition. They finally
made a home in the town of Onomichi, on the coast
of the Inland Sea. At nineteen, Fumiko left home to go to Tokyo, hoping to marry her fiancé.
Although she supported him with low-paying jobs, the family refused to approve the marriage,
and Fumiko was left on her own.

During these years, however, she began to write a poetic diary, which would eventually be-
come *Hōrōki (Diary of a Vagabond)*. She worked as a maid for the writer, Chikamasu Shūkō, and
then as a shop attendant, waitress, factory worker and in other positions. Hoping to become an
actress she arranged a meeting with the actor-poet Tanabe Wakao, and their relationship devel-
oped into a brief romantic affair. During the time she was with him, however, she made contact
with the modernist poetry circles, where her straightforward behavior and refusal to behave in
the role of a Japanese housewife, shocked some, but won friends of others.

The political and social discussions of these groups highly influenced her work. But the
poetry she created came distinctly from her own condition and spoke of her role, partly
fictionalized, partly based on fact, as an outsider. Linking her work to the plight of common
workers and the destitute, she forged a poetry that refused to defer to the patriarchal system of
Japan.

Diary of a Vagabond sold more than 600,000 copies upon its publication in 1930, and re-
sulted in her literary fame. Her other major work, *Aouma wo mitari (I Saw a Pale Horse)*, was
published in 1929.

BOOKS OF POETRY:

Aouma wo mitari (Tokyo: Nansō shoin, 1929); *Hōrōki* (1930); *Hayashi Fumiko zenshū*, Vol. 1
(Tokyo: Shinchōsha, 1951); *Hayashi Fumiko zenshū*, Vol. 2 (Tokyo: Sinchōsha, 1951).

ENGLISH LANGUAGE TRANSLATIONS:

I Saw a Pale Horse and Selected Poems from Diary of a Vagabond, trans. by Janice Brown (Ithaca,
New York: East Asia Program, Cornell University, 1997).

Under the Lantern

If you give me ten cups of King of Kings to drink
I shall throw you a kiss
ah, what a pitful waitress I am.

Outside the blue window, rain falls like drops of cut glass
under the light of the lantern
all has turned to wine.

Is Revolution the wind blowing north...?
I've spilled the wine
opening my red mouth over the spill on the table
I belch fire.

Shall I dance in my blue apron?
"Golden Wedding," or "Caravan"
tonight's dance music...

Still three more cups to go
How'm I doing? you ask
I'm just fine
although I'm a nice girl
a really nice girl
I scatter my feelings
generously like cut flowers
among petty pigs of men.
Ah, is Revolution the wind blowing north...?

—Translated from the Japanese by Janice Brown

(from *Aouma wo mitari*, 1929)

Taking Out the Liver

In the chicken liver fireworks scatter, and night comes
ladies and gentlemen! hear ye, hear ye!
the final scene with that man has come slowly but surely
in his bowels
sliced open with one sword cut
a killfish swims smartly.

It's a fetid, stinking night
if no one is home, I'll break in like a burglar!
I'm poor
and so that man has run away from me
it's a night that wraps me up in darkness.

—*Translated from the Japanese by Janice Brown*

(from *Aouma wo mitari*, 1929)

Red Sails Gone to Sea

Have you heard the sound of the tide?!
Have you heard the sound of the vast, wide sea?!

Entrusting the sooty lamps to their wives
the island factory workers kick pebbles along the beach
and gather on the sunset shore.

Have you heard the sound of the distant tide?!
Have you heard the voices of thousands of swarming human beings?!
This is a peaceful shipbuilding port on the Inland Sea
the narrow rows of houses on this island of Innoshima are
like the closed lids of seashells
trousers stained with oil and flags made of overalls are spread out
the sound of the factory gate being battered by brute force
that sound, wham, wham,
resounds over the whole island.

Whoooosh!
when the blue-painted service door is pushed by crowds of shoulders
the agile chameleons
holding account books colored with the blood and grease of the factory workers
jump nimbly into the launch
like foxes on a snowy night
From the factory workers' hardened faces twisted by emotion
tears of anquish gush
plop, plop, isn't that sound of the tears?
the fleeing launch
as it cuts in front of boats spread out like nets
then
the space between the fleeing launch and the workers thronging this small island
disappears in a single line of spray.

Even if they grit their teeth and rub their foreheads against the earth
the sky—
yesterday, today, too, it doesn't change
ordinary clouds stream past
Here!
The workers who have become crazy men, who have lost their heads
call the waves and howl at the sea
amidst the broken ships at the dock
they turn in a vortex and become an avalanche.

Have you heard the sound of the tide?!
Have you heard the sound of the distant waves?!
Wave the flags!

The vigorous young men
expose their shining skin
the cables whirring
straining with all they might at the ropes of the torn sails
they crash through the harbor gate
red sails set for the wind-howling sea!
Hey! Wave the flags!
Sing a song!
Though frayed and ragged
the red sails fill sturdily in the wind
kicking out white spray, they head to the sea!
Running like arrows to the middle of the ocean.

But...
hey, hey
calling out from the top of Storm God Mountain where the wind blows cold
prick up your ears at the shouts vigorous as the waves!
Poor wives and children
stand there on tiptoe
aren't they calling loudly to the sky, the sky!

Have you heard the sound of the distant tide?!
Have you heard the roar of the waves?!

Under the withered tree on the mountain
wives and children wave their hands together with the tree while deep in their eyes
the red sails are reflected forever
speeding along like sparks of fire.

> —*Translated from the Japanese by Janice Brown*

(from *Aouma wo mitari*, 1929)

Spread Out in the Sky the Cherry Tree Branches

Spread out in the sky the cherry tree branches
lightly stained blood-red
there! from the tips of the branches pink threads dangle
passion's lottery

Unable to make enough to eat, the dancing girl threw herself into vaudeville
and danced naked, even so
that's not the fault of the cherry blossoms.

One single emotion
brings double obligation
amidst the cherries gloriously blooming in the blue sky
strange threads reel in
the naked lips
of every
living woman.

Poor, young girls
at night
I've heard them throw their lips
into the heavens like fruit.

The rose-pink cherries coloring the blue sky
are the fated kisses of these lovely women
the traces of lips turned aside.

> —*Translated from the Japanese by Janice Brown*

(from *Hōrōki*, 1930)

Stubborn, Strong

Stubborn, strong
my poverty, my drinking, my pleasures
all those.
Ah, ah, ah

Slash them
knock them aside, send them flying
the things I've bewailed so many times, painful,
belching out art like spitting blood I shall dance and be happy like one mad.

—*Translated from the Japanese by Janice Brown*

(from *Hōrōki*, 1930)

I've Seen Fuji

I've seen Fuji
I've seen Mount Fuji
there was no red snow
so I need not praise Fuji as a fine mountain.

I'm not going to lose out to such a mountain
many times I've thought that,
seeing its reflection in the train window,
the heart of this peaked mountain
threatens my broken life
and looks down coldly on my eyes.

I've seen Fuji,
I've seen Mount Fuji
Birds!
Fly across that mountain from dome to peak
with your crimson mouths, give a scornful laugh
Wind!
Fuji is a great sorrowful palace of snow,
blow and rage
Mount Fuji is the symbol of Japan
it's a sphinx
a thick, dream-like nostalgia
a great, sorrowful palace of snow where demons live.

Look at Fuji,
Look at Mount Fuji
in your form painted by Hokusai
I have seen your youthful spark.

But now you're an old broken-down grave mound
always you turn your glaring eyes to the sky
why do you flee into the murky snow?

Birds, wind
rap on Mount Fuji's shoulder
so bright and still
it's not a silver citadel
it's a great, sorrowful palace of snow that hides misfortune.

Mount Fuji!
Here stands a lone woman who does not lower her head to you
here is a woman laughing scornfully at you.

Mount Fuji, Fuji
your passion like rustling fire
howls and roars
until you knock her stubborn head down
I shall wait, happily whistling.

—*Translated from the Japanese by Janice Brown*

(from *Hōrōki*, 1930)

Early Evening Light

Early evening light   I sleep quietly on evening islands
at the bottom of the sea throngs of fish
murmuring softly in elegant voices
whisperings of fish, jealousy of fish.
From a distant place the setting sun appears
above the earth, heralding the single paper layer of night
human beings moan in their sleep
evening islands   evening light

Soldiers leave their villages
students return to their homes
in their lives people moan
murmuring, it's my problem, too
is there peace in the world?
it's the feeling of hard, sticky sweets
what is human life, I wonder...
the torture continues
human beings sharing the torment.
Sooner or later these islands will disappear
only cows and chickens will survive
these two animals will interbreed
cows will grow feathers
and cockscombs
birds will grow horns
and cowtails.
Is there such a thing as eternity?
Eternity is the wind blowing beside your ear
evening light   islands merely floating
shaking like a baby carriage
archaeologists, too, perish in the end...

—Translated from the Japanese by Janice Brown

(from *Hōrōki*, 1930)

The Fat Moon Has Vanished

The fat moon has vanished
carried off by a devil
hats on their heads everyone looked up at the sky.
A person licking his fingers
someone smoking a pipe
children shouting
in the dark sky the wind howls.

A lonely cough resonates from someone's windpipe
the blacksmith kindles his fire
the moon has gone somewhere.
Hail falls the size of spoons
the wrangling begins.

On a wager we went to look for the moon
and it's been tossed into a stove somewhere,
people clamor and shout.
Now, how long will it be
before people forget the moon and go on living?

—Translated from the Japanese by Janice Brown

(from *Hōrōki*, 1930)

PERMISSIONS

"Under the Lantern," "Taking Out the Liver," "Red Sails Gone to Sea," "Spread Out in the Sky the Cherry Tree Branches," "Stubborn, Strong," "I've Seen Fuji," "Early Evening Light," and "The Fat Moon Has Vanished"
Reprinted from *I Saw a Pale Horse and Selected Poems from Diary of a Vagabond*, trans. by Janice Brown (Ithaca, New York: East Asia Program, Cornell University, 1997). Copyright ©1997 by Janice Brown. Reprinted by permission of Janice Brown.

Frigyes Karinthy (Hungary)
1887–1938

Frigyes Karinthy was a prolific writer of short stories, poetry, plays, and essays. But he is best known as a humorist and satirist, the author of sequels to Swift's *Gulliver's Travels* — *Utazás Feremidóba* (1916, Journey to Faremído) and *Capillaria* (1921) — and the autobiographical *Utazás a koponyám Körül* (1937, Journey Around My Skull). His poetry — often a blend of Biblical-like diction and colloquial language or, as one critic has described it, "a mixture of carefully polished...classical language and broadly-rolling, Whitmanesque verse" — was collected in *Nam mondhatom al senkinek* (1930, I Cannot Tell it to Anyone) and *Üzenet a palaaaackban* (1938, Message in a Bottle).

In Hungary he is also beloved as the author of a book of parodies, *Így írtok to* (This Is How YOU Write), many of whose lines have become proverbial. Like many of the New York Alonquin writers in the United States, Karinthy became known as a wit of almost legendary repute. With writer Dezsű Kosztolányi, he held literary court at the famed Budapest New York Café, as he and Kosztolányi played sophisticated verbal games and satirized the leading Hungarian poets such as Endre Ady, Mihály Babits, Gyula Illyés, Attila József and Lőrinc Szabó. Karinthy's son, the noted novelist Ferenc Karinthy, contributed to the stories surrounding of his father.

BOOKS OF POETRY:

Nem mondhatom el senkinek (1930); *Üzenet a palackban* (1938)

ENGLISH LANGUAGE TRANSLATIONS:

Selections in *In Quest of the Miracle Stag: The Poetry of Hungary*, edited by Adam Makkai (Chicago: Atlantis Centaur/Budapest: Corvina, 1996).

The Message in the Bottle
(*The Poet Is Asked Why He No Longer Writes Poems*)

(a few illegible lines, then:)
...my fingers
are frozen. This bottle's in my left hand. The right
holds the joystick. It has grown very stiff.
There's thick ice on the wings. I don't
know whether the engine can take it. It makes Queer
snoring noises in here. It's terribly cold.
I don't know how high up I am
(or how deep? or how far?)
Nearness and distance — all empty. And all
my instruments are frozen: the scales
of Lessing and the compressometer of the Academy;
the Martinetti altimeter, too. I think
I must be high enough because the penguins
no longer lift their heads as my propeller
drones above them, cutting across
the Northern Lights. They no longer hear me. Here are
no signs to see. Down there's some rocky land. New land?
Unknown? Ever explored before? By whom? Perhaps
by Scott? Strinderg? Byron? Leopardi?
I don't know. And I confess
I don't care. I'm cold, the taste
of this thin air is bitter, horribly bitter...
It could be that my nose has started to bleed.
I'm hungry... I've eaten all my biscuits.
Some unknown star keeps blinking
at the point I gaze at. The pemmican
has gone maggoty... What star can that be?
Perhaps already... from the beyond...? And what's the date?
Wednesday? Thursday? Or New Year's Eve? Who could be
sitting around the homely hearth? Little brothers,
singing birds,
beside the anxiously guarded hearth
of petty feelings; bird brothers in the depths
of the human heart's jungle... Hallo! Hallo!
Is there no one to hear this exiled fellow-crow, myself?
A little while ago
something crackled through the rusty antenna of my radio...
I hear that Mr. D. has found a fine adjective
in Banality Harbor

while C. has discovered a new metaphor
between two rhymes in Love Canal.
The Society's reporting it. Congratulations!
I'll...tell you all...that I...
when I get home...and...land...
all that I...felt up here...only when
he escapes....can....the traveler....relate it....
But how does he every escape to return?
Now I put these few confused lines
into the empty wine bottle
and drop it through the hatch. Like rolling dice!
If an uncouth pearl-diver should find it, let him
throw it away, a broken oyster,
bt should a literate sailor find it,
I send this message through him:
    "Here I am, at the Thirteenth Latitude of Desolation,
the Hundredth Longitude of Shame,
the utmost Altitude of teeth-gnashing Defiance,
somewhere far out, at the point of the Ultimate,
and still I wonder whether it is possible
to go any farther..."

—Translated from the Hungarian by Paul Tabori

Dandelion

Towards your hand,
Towards your hand, your hair
Towards your hand, your hair, your eyes
Towards your hand, your hair, your eyes, your skirt
Why this snatching? — You ask me always,
Annoyed and loudly, or shaking your head in silence —

Why not soft and gentle caresses,
Yes, well behaved, like others would do it.
Why this snatching, and in my eyes a twinkle
And worse still, I am laughing — impudently!
It is so strident, rude and ear-splitting!
You'll leave me here at once, or smack my hand!
Flower, don't leave me, I rather tell you
I tell you — I breathe in your ear, wait,
Just smooth this curl away now.

Towards your hand,
Towards your hand, your hair
Towards your hand, your hair, your eyes
Towards your hand, your hair, your eyes, your skirt
What keeps snatching — you still cannot remember?
What keeps snatching — you still can't think of it? —
Though you've this same expression
Always when, annoyed, you try to fend it off
Holding your hair, your eyes, your skirt against it.

Towards your stem
Towards your stem stamen
Towards your stem stamen pistil
Towards your stem stamen pistil petals
What keeps snatching, flower? — The wind!
The wind, the wind, impudent, fickle wind
Chirping cheerfully, seeing you annoyed.

Flower, what next?
This was just a light breeze
This can only snatch and chirp away,
But now I have to speak to you about my family,
Listen, I say!
Proud, Trumpeting Tempest was my father —
      The famous Typhoon of Arkansas my mother,
A whirling tornado married my sister —
Fair flowerfluff, have you ever wallowed exalted — exhausted
Hoisted on a heaven-piercing hurricane?
So don't smack me now on the hand, dear.

—Translated from the Hungarian by Peter Zollman

Struggle for Life

Brother, it seems, you have been beaten.
As Law decrees and Precept goes —
Your corpse is sniffed round by hyenas
And circled by the hungry crows.

It's not the pack who were the stronger,
Smaller beasts beat you to tatters —
And who fights now over your carcass:
Jackdaw? Jackal? Hardly matters.

Your fist when it was time to use it
Always stopped halfway in the air —
Was it Charity? Weakness? May be.
Fear? Pride? Modesty? I don't care.

Or mere disgust, perhaps. So be it.
Good. Amen, I accept the terms.
I prefer that worms should eat me
Rather than I should feed on worms.*

—*Translated from the Hungarian by Peter Zollman*

PERMISSIONS

"The Message in the Bottle," "Dandelion," and "Struggle for Life"
Reprinted from *In Quest of the Miracle Stag: The Poetry of Hungary*, edited by Adam Makkai (Chicago:
Atlantis Centaur/Budapest: Covina, 1996). Copyright ©1996 by Atlantis-Centaur. Reprinted by permission
of Adam Makkai, with thanks to Peter Zollman and Paul Tabori.

---

* These two lines have become proverbial in Hungarian.

Artur Lundkvist [Sweden]
1906–1991

Born into modest circumstances in Hagstad, Swe-
den, Artur Lundkvist was primarily self-educated;
over the years he learned to read over a dozen lan-
guages and traveled extensively.

His first book of poetry, *Glöd* (1928, Embers) was
a celebration of life, as were most of his works
throughout the 1930s. But the 1936 book *Nattens
broar* (The Bridges of Night) and *Sirensång* (Siren
Song) of the following year both represent the
influence of Surrealism upon his work.

The years of World War II and after saw an in-
creasing attention to narrative, expressed by
Lundkvist brilliantly in the prose poem, particularly
Agadir (1961), which describes the 1960 earthquake
that struck the Moroccoan city.

Lundkvist also wrote extensively about his travel and brought back to Sweden his excite-
ment about world writers such as William Faulkner, Pablo Neruda and Czesław Miłosz.

In 1968 he was voted a member of the Swedish Academy. In 1981 Lundkvist suffered a heart
attack during a lecture and lay in a coma for sixty days. Upon his recovery, he wrote the halluci-
natory experiences of the subconscious, *Färdas i drömmen och föreställningen* (1984, *Journeys in
Dream and Imagination*).

BOOKS OF POETRY:

Glöd (Stockholm: Albert Bonniers Förlag, 1928); Naket liv (Stockholm: Albert Bonniers Förlag,
1929); *Svart stad* (Stockholm: Albert Bonniers Förlag, 1930); *Vit Man* (Stockholm: Albert Bonniers
Förlag, 1932); *Nattens broar* (Stockholm: Albert Bonniers Förlag, 1936); *Sirensång* (Stockholm:
Albert Bonniers Förlag, 1937); *Eldtema* (Stockholm: Albert Bonniers Förlag, 1939); *Korsväg*
(Stockholm: Albert Bonniers Förlag, 1942); *Skinn över sten* (Stockholm: Albert Bonniers Förlag,
1947); *Fotspår i vattnet* (Stockholm: Albert Bonniers Förlag, 1949); *Liv som gräs* (Stockholm:
Albert Bonniers Förlag, 1954); *Vindrosor Moteld* (Stockholm: Albert Bonniers Förlag, 1955); *Det
talande trädet* (Stockholm: Albert Bonniers Förlag, 1960); *Agadir* (Stockholm: Tiden, 1961);
Ögonblick och vågor (Stockholm: Albert Bonniers Förlag, 1962); *Texter i snön* (Stockholm: Albert
Bonniers Förlag, 1964); *Mörkskogen* (Stockholm: Albert Bonniers Förlag, 1967); *Brottställen*
(Stockholm: Albert Bonniers Förlag, 1968); *Snapphanens liv och död* (Stockholm: Albert Bonniers
Förlag, 1968); *Besvärjelser till tröst* (Stockholm: Albert Bonniers Förlag, 1969); *Långt borta, mycket
nära* (Goteborg: Författarförlaget, 1970); *Lustgårdens demoni* (Stockholm: Albert Bonniers Förlag,
1973); *Fantasins slott och vardagens stenar* (Goteborg: Författarförlaget, 1974); *Livet i ögat*
(Stockholm: Albert Bonniers Förlag, 1970); *Världens härlighet* (Stockholm: Albert Bonniers
Förlag, 1975); *Krigarens dikt* (Stockholm: Albert Bonniers Förlag, 1976); *Flykten och överlevandet*
(Stockholm: Albert Bonniers Förlag, 1977); *Skrivet mot kvällen* (Stockholm: Albert Bonniers

Förlag, 1980); *Sinnebilder* (Stockholm: Albert Bonniers Förlag, 1982); *Färdas i drömmen och föreställningen* (Stocklholm: Albert Bonniers Förlag, 1984).

ENGLISH LANGUAGE TRANSLATIONS:

Agadir, trans. by William Jay Smith and Leif Sjöberg (Athens: Ohio University Press, 1979); *The Talking Tree: Poems in Prose*, trans. by Diana W. Wormuth with Steven P. Sondrup (Provo, Utah: Brigham Young University Press, 1982); *Journeys in Dream and Imagination*, trans. by Ann B. Weissman and Annika Planck (New York: Four Walls Eight Windows, 1991).

To Maria

I wish you a room papered with block prints from Ethiopia and a necklace made of snail shells still inhabited by purple snails, a wheelbarrow full of sunflowers and a pine brewing aromatic coffee outside your window.

It is in the painful summertime when the dogrose closes its eye, the hard summertime with the nests without eggs, when you shy away in the twilight under the whitebeams, when the brook whispers good night in the middle of the day, where you glimpse the too-white calf and the dog with his inside-out skin.

I wish you teeth of diamond, pain-free forever and eyes that bathe in the Titicaca of clear panoramas, I wish you a summerhouse made of playing cards and lilies of the valley and a black chest furnished as a little bar with neon lighting and a needle with eyes in both ends like two sisters with their feet towards each other in the same bed.

A woman formed in the sand was found in the morning covered with prints of birds' feet, the world's largest dog comes and licks the bird-shaped birthmark on your knee, a white raven writes the opening lines to your next poem, and a summer wave says it wants to carry you into November.

I wish you a bed with adjustable dream-wishes and a ladybug that embroiders in silver on black sheets, a butterfly that flies out of Hans Christian Andersen's long nose and shows the way to a house made of grass in the forest, where all the hidden secrets turn inside out, where that which does not yet exist waits to be born, where disappointments are changed into fulfillment, and a rose keeps watch under your sleeping cheek.

Do you still stay with the bird that extends its wings without flying, the bird that sings about the egg inside the bird and the bird inside the egg, free in itself and prisoner in others, just as your enemy rests in you as your best friend as you wander restlessly about in the painful summer?

Finally I wish you a wing to carry you over stones and thickets, beyond stone throws and dog barks, beyond traps and shots, and lift you like a swing without dizziness high over the tree tops on your birthday.

—*Translated from the Swedish by Diana W. Wormuth in collaboration with Steven P. Sondrup*

Relativity

There is nothing large or small except in our imagination. The tiger lets himself be frightened by a frog. The ant climbs directly into the crocodile's open jaws.

There is no up or down. That depends only on the situation we find ourselves in. He who stands on his head an hour a day knows that.

I, the master, say that. There is no wet or dry. The sea is its own desert, the desert its own sea. There are springs hidden in a grain of sand. There are deserts of dryness between the drops of the sea.

There is no good or evil. There is a chain which rattles past without end, its links are made up of good and evil and are interlocked with one another. If one destroys this chain, one destroys the world. I, the master, say that.

There is no round or flat, no globe or surface. Everything curves in on itself, we only notice that we do not notice.

Knowledge is a burden. Where there is knowledge, there is no liberation. Thought and feeling rest heavily over each other, alternately. He who knows cannot understand. He who feels cannot realize. He who sits cannot walk. Everything which is itself suffers for not being something else. The done is not undone, the undone is not done and can never become that.

I, the master, say that.

He who creates cannot rest. Creation continues and pulls its creator with it. The crime grows wider, but does not cease by widening.

A handful of emptiness would be able to dislodge the universe. But where could one get hold of a handful of emptiness?

The balance is delicate, but the balance's possibilities are far drawn out. A lapel pin can counterbalance a six-story building, a straw hat a full-grown elephant. It depends on their placement in relation to each other.

The boat sinks when the reeds hide it, no glances hold it up longer.

Naked man frightens the fur-covered animals, they do not recognize themselves in him.

The warrior carries his sword until it bores through him. The pious man carries his cross until it takes root in him.

The sick man carries health with him like a flask of water. The prisoner draws the cage around himself. The free man also dupes freedom and leaves it behind him.

I, the master, say that. There is no past or future. The past tastes of future, the future tastes of the past, like the same water at two different times of the day. Only the river exists, without beginning or end.

—Translated from the Swedish by Diana W. Wormuth in collaboration with Steven P. Sondrup

The Wheel Book

It looks like an irregular globe or a kind of clumsy wheel left at the side of the road as if after an accident.

But when you come closer, you see that it is neither a globe nor a wheel but an unknown object you have never seen before. It has a certain resemblance to a book, seems to consist of tightly pressed pages which extend out in all directions almost in the form of a globe or a wheel.

You turn this book, globe, or book wheel over and over, all too interested to be able to leave it to its fate at once. It turns out to be alike on all sides, without the least opening between the pages, a completely closed book (if it is a book).

It is too heavy and shapeless to lift, possibly you could roll it with you, it even seems intended for that. If you could open it, it would be high enough so that you could read it comfortably sitting, while turning it around as you read.

But however you try, this book (if it really is a book) is still completely inaccessible, impossible to open, only page stuck to page, running around unchanging, and finally you must give up the hope of finding an opening where you can begin to read.

Then you get the idea of getting an axe and attacking the book, it's not going to slip away from you so easily. You chop and the axe blade fastens in the packed mass of paper, it is hard to get it loose again after each chop. When you finally manage to make an opening and get some bits of paper loose, it is a disappointment: only white paper and nothing to read!

—*Translated from the Swedish by Diana W. Wormuth in collaboration with Steven P. Sondrup*

from *Journeys in Dream and Imagination*

It is the dog returning, the same dog or a different one, a shadow dog I cannot clearly perceive, it has no definite form or color, approaches me somewhat threateningly, with a purpose, but then it becomes uncertain, hesitates, lies down or turns around, starts walking away, but remains silent,

maybe it is quite harmless, just seems to want something without knowing what, maybe it is looking for company or a stroking hand, someone who will talk to it, someone who will treat it as a human being,

it might be an unfortunate soul imprisoned in its fur, in its dog-like apparition, it keeps approaching me, maybe hoping each time that I am the human it is looking for, the one who will recognize it and give it a right to exist,

the dog remains totally silent, does not yelp or whine, maybe so as not to disturb me or even frighten me, or maybe it has no voice,

should I do something for this dog, attempt to call it close to me, reach out to stroke its fur...but I am not particularly fond of dogs and I do not quite trust this dog in spite of the compassion that eventually fills me,

I try to talk to it when it approaches me again, but no, it is more apprehensive than before, it is as if it wants me there, but immobile and silent, sometimes it disappears after a while as if prematurely giving up even trying to come close, it may not show up for two or three days, and then it returns as if nothing had happened,

this dog confuses me more and more, we have nothing in common and yet, there seems to already be some kind of connection between us, as if, against my wishes, I have become its lord and master, responsible for its destiny, as if it were a part of my own destiny

A gate, a gate! I see it in front of me, a gate in a high wall as around an old city, a gate that is still open, I can see that from a distance, a gate one must reach at the very last moment, before it is inexorably closed for the night or perhaps forever,

I hurry as much as I can, still running although I am losing my breath, my heart beats furiously in my chest, blood flows through my limbs so that my hands feel like stuffed gloves,

I probably will not make it in time, I despair about it but still continue my effort to the utmost, but if I do not arrive there before the gate is closed, I mgiht just as well fall in front of it, and I am lying there as if dead, one arm still lifted to pound on the gate,

but in vain, meaningless, since the gate is of iron and there is not the smallest window or opening in the wall so that someone might see me

You can see flocks of birds against the spring sky, pollen edges the riverbanks with yellow, a silken black bird with wheat-colored beak follows the shorelines and sings, like a master of treetops, also showing the direction of the wind,

there are the tall ones, the blond and reddish ones, with eyes blue as lakes and sky, hands with calloused grips and hair like sparse grain on the body,

they are like gods singed by fire, grandiose, bragging, power-charged, urinating like stallions, contemptuous of the renegades who flocked to the pale god or to Ulfila, for them rather skulls of horses carried on lances, tails of horses fluttering in the wind between tents of skins and sails of skins,

the oars are smeared with honey so as not to squeak and creak, smoke gives taste and smell to man and follows him like the fresh tar and the white birch bark around the dwellings with groups of swine and poultry, there are rotating grindstones and stone mills already invented and brought along for the journey,

the art of smithing is half secret, its masters living in caves, at hearths with fire, shrunken to dwarfs and enlarged to giants, strings are strung between bows of trees, with harmonies plucked by the wind like wildflowers, fire lives in the flint, knife-sharp, and attracts lightning,

the shores of the sea yield amber that is gall-green stomachs cannot digest, like petrified sunshine from the darkness of depth, for ornaments between women's breasts and on wrists, with a fly caught in the amber as a small miracle to gaze upon in a streak of sun that shines through the fingers making them wine red,

the long boats are buried in the earth with their chieftains to never more tempt them to break up and travel, the settled ones anchored by rocks and tree trunks

—*Translated from the Swedish by Ann B. Weissmann and Annika Planck*

Jackson Mac Low [U S A]
1922

Poet, composer, essayist, performance artist, play-wright, and painter, Jackson Mac Low was born in Chicago in 1922. His poetry began to be published in 1941. Since 1954 he has often employed chance operations and other nonintentional, as well as intentional techniques, when composing verbal, musical, theatrical, and multimedia performance works. Mac Low's turn to nonintentional methods was inspired by Zen Buddhism (as taught by Dr. D.T. Suzuki), the *I Ching*, and John Cage and his music composed in the early 1950s by chance operations, some of which is indeterminate in its performance.

By the middle 1960s, Mac Low was well known for his readings, performances, and theater works. *The Marrying Maiden*, a play chance-operationally derived (1958–59) from the *I Ching*, was performed by The Living Theater in New York in 1960–1961; it was directed by Judith Malina, with decor by Julian Beck and music by John Cage. Mac Low's *Verdurous Sanguinaria* (written in 1961 and published in 1967) premiered in 1961, produced by the composer La Monte Young in Yoko Ono's New York loft. His *Twin Plays* was performed in 1963. Selections from *The Pronouns*, forty poems that are instructions for dancers, was written in 1964 and performed in 1965 by Meredith Monk and a group she organized.

In 1963, with the editor, La Monte Young, Mac Low co-published the first edition of *An Anthology*, which through George Maciunas gave rise to Fluxus, of which Mac Low was the first literary editor. Mac Low published several books of poetry throughout the 1960s and 1970s, including *August Light Poems* (1967), *22 Light Poems* (1968), *Stanzas for Iris Lezak* (1972), *4 trains* (1974), *21 Matched Asymmetries* (1978), and *Asymmetries 1–260* (1980).

The 1980s saw Mac Low working more often in intentional poetic forms, influenced, in part, by the "Language" poets, some of whom themselves claimed Mac Low's poetry as an influence. Among the major works of this period are *From Pearl Harbor Day to FDR's Birthday* (1982) and *Bloomsday* (1984). A large selection of his work also appeared in *Representative Works: 1938–1985* (1986). Over the past decade Mac Low has continued to publish important works including *Twenties* (1991), *Pieces O' Six* (1992), and *42 Merzgedichte* in Memoriam *Kurt Schwitters*, which won the 1994 America Award for the best new book of American poetry. In 1999 Mac Low was awarded the Tanning Prize for Poetry.

BOOKS OF POETRY:

The Pronouns—A Collection of 40 Dances—for the Dancers (New York: Mac Low and Judson Dance Workshop, 1964); *August Light Poems* (New York: Caterpillar Books, 1967); *22 Light Poems* (Los Angeles: Black Sparrow Books, 1968); *Stanzas for Iris Lezak* (Barton, Vermont: Something Else Press, 1972); *4 trains* (Providence, R. I.: Burning Deck, 1974); *36th Light Poem: In Memoriam Buster Keaton* (London: Permanent Press, 1975); *21 Matched Asymmetries* (London:

Aloes Books, 1978); *phone* (New York and Amsterdam: Printed Editions and Kontexts, 1979); *Asymmetries 1–260* (New York: Printed Editions, 1980); *"Is that Wool Hat My Hat?"* (Milwaukee: Membrane Press, 1982); *From Pearl Harbor Day to FDR's Birthday* (Los Angeles: Sun & Moon Press, 1982); *Bloomsday* (Barrytown, N.Y.: Station Hill, 1984); *French Sonnets* (Black Mesa, 1984); *The Virginia Woolf Poems* (Providence, R.I.: Burning Deck, 1985); *Representative Works: 1938–1985* (New York: Roof Books, 1986); *Words nd Ends from Ez* (Bolinas, California: Avenue B, 1989); *Twenties: 100 Poems* (New York: Roof Books, 1991); *Pieces o' Six* (Los Angeles: Sun & Moon Press, 1992); *42 Merzgedichte* in Memoriam *Kurt Schwitters* (Barrytown, N.Y.: Station Hill, 1994); *Barnesbook* (Los Angeles: Sun & Moon Press, 1996).

Selections from "The 11th of July"
(19 Cub Lot Poems New York, 11 July 1946)

HEAR I HERE

Hear I here I hear!
In between the between in between.
I listen. no. no. no.

Here I hear I here!
Between the between!
I here!

No. no. no.

Between the hear the here!
No. no. no. Hear!
The between.

MEMORY

Cleats, cleavages, the freedom, the freedom;
Horns on the haunted, the hinted;
Clatters of Christians flintly.
The Cleavages.

Memory (the cleavages) memory.
I hint I hunt.

Memory eagerness memory,
I hint I hunt I hear.

Memory memory memory
The cleavages!

Memory

CLEAR REAPERS PLEASING

Clear reapers pleasing.
Help the heed the, heedful.
Clear reapers pleasing.
Help the herd the, heard.
Clear reapers pleasing.

& THE

At tear the & when the & when the.
And.

At tear the & when the at tear the:
And the at, where,

At the.

And the at, tear the, and the,
At the at tear the at the
And the when the (where), and the,

& the.

11 July 1946
New York

(from *Representative Works*, 1986)

September Pack

Overflame arctic.

Foundried once
glass will fusion chill
yet.

Flaunt orange of sun bone
thirds.

More and bequeathes glacial need the fungoid joiners
and several yet fiery gray nascent friends skin Cimabue ashes
dear come high isle lucence morning tinkling consumed purgation
more solar the thanks
metallophonic scarlet from so
O leafmeal of
no
foliage milieus more
me anxiety tan vitrous
a a to red when shades conduct
deeper.

Of in through glinting aborning seracs
when
gleams.

Khaki yet.

Pipe perfection the and toll sublime
to.

Geysers once.

25 September 1959
The Bronx

(from *Representative Works*, 1986)

16th Dance—Being Red Enough—21 February 1964

Somebody boils delicate things,
& afterwards, being in flight
& doing something consciously,
somebody's going about & coming across art.

Then somebody doing something under the conditions of
    competition
rails
& gets.

Later somebody seems to keep a rod under a bit of cushion.

Then giving a bit or doing something elastic,
somebody gives an egg to someone loose or seems to do so
& shocks somebody,
making a structure with a roof or under a roof
& doing things with the mouth & eyes
& finally damaging something foolish.

(from *The Pronouns*, 1964)

A Lack of Balance But Not Fatal

A motion guided a lotion
in hiding from a tint
reckless from nowhere enforcement.

A label persisted. The past tense
implies it took place. The redness
in which the the implies there was some other
did not persist. He was not waiting long.

The sentence is not always a line
but the stanza is a paragraph.

The whiteness was not enforced.
It was not the other but another
circumstance brought in the waterfall
while a breath waited without being clear
or even happier. A seal was lost without it.

There was a typical edge. The paper tilted
or even curved. A rattle smoothed its way.
Where the predominance stopped was anyone's guess
but the parrot fought for it with forbearance
and a waiting cart was leashed to a trial
though a lie would have done as well
or even better when a moderate sleeve was cast.

No claim was made. A tired park gained.
A lack twisted the bread. Heads foamed.
Nowhere was little enough for the asking.
The task he cleared from the temperature
was outside the extended account. Each the
points to an absence. One or more hiding.

He asked where the inches were. The could have gone.

Intentions are mixed without quotations.
The song was snug. Ambiguity does not
hang in the air. The space between graphemes
is neither colorless nor tasteless. A stream
runs rapidly in no more history. The sweep
of a line. Kindness is not mistaken
for tinder and the lid is resting but shortness
guarantees no sentence authenticity.

Where the schoolyard was evident a closed
flutter showed a notion without resistant
fences or a paradox without feathers.
Swiftness outlasts the pencil. A cormorant
rose against a born backdrop. Letters inch.
An iconoclast was hesitant. A fire lit.
In the tank a lozenge disengages. Swarms
roared. A special particle felt its form.
Lagging features left oak divination without
a tone or a creased sentinel. Leavings swept.

Toward evening the watchful clock was situated.
No diver called for ether. Lynxes thrived.
Hit by something a silence willed. Streets
were not concerned. A past participle's
sometimes mistaken for a past. An orange
roster was on everybody's mind though clues
could be found. When the ink is incomplete
every table rests on its opposite. A closed
restraint impinged. Furniture rested. Several
pinks in a fist. A clearly charismatic
hideout was read. Neatness wavered. The flag
was wet without exertion or favor. That judge postponed.

Snowfall abused ermines. A folding chair.
Close to the bank a trap was silted though the finder
relaxed without particulars or the least inclination.
Whoever loosed the torrent concluded the tryst.
Finally is the way to find the place. Earshot
is likely. Tones harvest commonplace weather.
The pastness of the past was included in a doctrine
or stakes were wrought. Or sought. Find divers.
Fists rested on the divined peculiarity. Artemis hushed.

Twigs were not grapes. He grasped the talc ring.
Smoothing the horses the clutter died. Finches
sewed roses on the mustered aggregate. Loaves flew.
A mentality ran farther and its crests simmered.
Closeted without bargains the lean rump beheld
no future. A certain flight beckoned. The wonder.
Closed classrooms risk warmth though causation
matters less. Never ink a connection when a plea
is off. Softer dollars were a range without flutters
though a concessive subordinator turns a sentence
into a scene. Dreams were not what he wanted.

16 January 1982
New York

(from *From Pearl Harbor Day to FDR's Birthday*, 1982)

Giant Otters

They were a close family of giant otters
in Surinam giving a low growling sound when
they were insecure so they were called the Hummers.

Trace elements had landed near them and they effloresced
in even amounts throughout an even eon and an evening more
fortunate as they were in knowing nothing

or peering curiously into unknowable presence
alert to no future living the past as presence
whose elements were traces in their efflorescing being

going as far as they could within the world they were
as fortune particularized occasions within unfolding
breathed upon by memory's wraith and anticipation's all but absence.

Where were they going but farther along and through
whatever their being eventuated in clearness no demand for clarity
as the eyes are unsealed and the world flows in as light?

13–14 February 1982
New York

(from *Bloomsday*, 1984)

PERMISSIONS

"Selections from 'The 11ᵗʰ of July'" and "September Pack"
Reprinted from *Representative Works: 1938–1985* (New York: Roof Books, 1986). Copyright ©1986 by Jackson Mac Low. Reprinted by permission of Roof Books.

"16ᵗʰ Dance—Being Red Enough—21 February 1964"
Reprinted from *The Pronous: A Collection of Forty Dancers for the Dancers*, (Barrytown, New York: Station Hill, 1979). Copyright ©1979 by Jackson Mac Low. Reprinted by permissionof Station Hill.

Osip Mandelshtam [Russia]
1891–1938

Osip Mandelshtam grew up in St. Petersburg in an assimilated middle-class, Jewish family. He was educated in classical studies at the Tenishev School.

From 1907–1910 Mandelshtam spent most of his time in western Europe, where he discovered the French Symbolists and other contemporary writing of his time. In 1911, he returned to Russia, attending St. Petersburg University. There he joined with poets Anna Akhmatova and Nikolai Gumilyov in establishing the poetic movement, Acmeism.

Mandelshtam continued to write during World War I and the Russian Revolution, taking no active role in either conflict. During the civil war he served briefly in the Education Ministry in Moscow under Anatoly Lunacharsky.

Mandelshtam's early works include *Kamen* (1913, *Stone*) and *Tristia* (1922). After 1922, he was unable to publish until the end of the decade. During that time he supported himself by translating and writing children's books. In 1928 he published *Stikhotvorenia 1921–25* (*Poems 1921–25*), containing some of his most important and profound meditations. In 1934 he was arrested by Stalin for denouncing him as a "peasant slayer," and was sentenced to three years exile in Voronezh. At the end of that time, he was allowed to return to Moscow, but was eventually banished to the suburbs. He was arrested again in May of 1938, and this time he was sentenced to five years hard labor. In a transit camp near Vladivostok, he died of heart failure.

BOOKS OF POETRY:

Kamen (1913); *Tristia* (1922); *Stikhotvorenia 1921–25* (1928); *Sobranie sochinenii* (4 volumes), edited by Gleb Struve and Boris Filipoff (Vol 1: Washington, D.C.: Inter-Language Library Associates, 1964; Vol 2: Washington, D.C.: Inter-Langauge Associates, 1966; Vol 3: Washington, D.C.: Inter-Language Literary Associates, 1979; Vol 4: Paris: YMCA Press, 1981); *Stikhotvoreniia*, Edited by Nikolai I. Khardzhiev (Leningrad: Biblioteka poeta, 1974).

ENGLISH LANGUAGE TRANSLATIONS:

Osip Mandelstam's "Stone," translated by Robert Tracy (Princeton, N.J.: Princeton University Press, 1981); *Osip Mandelstam: Selected Poems*, translated by Clarence Brown and W. S. Merwin (Oxford/New York: Oxford Univrsity Press/Athenaeum, 1973/1974); *Osip Mandelstam: 50 Poems*, translated by Bernard Meares (New York: Persea Books, 1977); *Osip Mandelstam: Selected Poems*, translated by David McDuff (Cambridge: Cambridge University Press, 1974); *Osip Manselstam: Poems Chosen and Translated by James Green* (Boulder, CO: Shambhala Publications, 1978); *A Necklace of Bees: Selected Poems*, translated by Maria Enzensberger (London: The Menard Press, 1992).

Insomnia

Insomnia. Homer. Taut sails.
I have read the list of ships to the middle:
this migrant flight
that once winged over Hellas.

What drives this wedge of cranes into alien borders?
What do you seek, Archean men?
Were it not for Helen,
What need had you of Troy?

Homer falls silent
And foam swirls from the heads of kings.
Only the black sea rages
And a heavy surf thunders against my pillow.

—*Translated from the Russian by John Glad*

(from *Kamen*, 1915)

On Stony Pierian Spurs

On stony Pierian spurs
the muses' ring was forged in dance
that blind bards might lay up for us like bees
heavy combs of Ionian honey.
And from the bulging female brow
fell coldness
that distant grandsons might touch
the archipelago's tender coffins.

Spring tramples the fields of Hellas
as Sappho pulls on a red slipper.
And from the cicada's hidden smithy
tiny hammers ring out over the cut grass.
Already beef hides have been stretched
over wedding shoes,
and before the carepenter's door
scamper headless chickens.

Turtle-like
the lyre lies fingerless,
baking its golden belly
in the Epirian sun.
She longs to be flipped over, caressed.
Where is Terpander?
How long must she wait
for the rape of dry thumbs?

Above the gossiping, bare-headed grass
wasps copulate with honeysuckle
and oaks drink deep from tepid springs.
I would break no bread
and sip but wine and honey
where the creak of labor
does not blacken the islands' sky.

—Translated from the Russian by John Glad

(from *Tristia*, 1922)

Can't remember how long
This song's been know to me—
Does a thief slink along to its tune
Or the prince of mosquitoes drone?

I would like just one more time
To speak of nothing at all,
To blaze up like a match in the dark,
Or nudge night awake with my shoulder.

To lift off the air's hat
Like a smothering haystack,
To shake up a heavy sack
Chock-full of caraway seeds.

So that the flow of blood
And the ringing of dry grass
Ever after would ripple on
Through the ages, the hayloft, the dream.

—Translated from the Russian by Maria Enzensberger

(from *Stikhotvorenia 1921-25*, 1928)

I Am Deaf

I am deaf,
I am blind,
From my ears trickle ochre and minium,
In my eyes well rust and vermilion.

I dream
Of Armenian mornings.
I wonder,
How do bluebirds live in Yerevan?

I see a baker
Playing blindman's bluff with bread,
Lifting the moist skins of lavash cakes
From a hearth.

Oh Yerevan, Yerevan!
Did a bird draw you?
Or did a childish lion
Color you with crayons?

Oh Yerevan, Yerevan!
You're not a town,
You're a walnut,
How I love the crooked Bablyons of your streets!

I have fingered this senseless life
Like a mullah his Koran.
I've frozen time
And spilled no hot blood.

Oh, Yerevan.
That's enough.
Anway,
I don't want your frozen grapes.

—*Translated from the Russian by John Glad*

(1930)

Leningrad

I'm back in my town — excruciatingly familiar
as a child's glands.
Hurriedly I gulp the river lights' fishy grease
and recognize the yolk of a December day
spilling into an evil tar.
Petersburg, I don't want to die!
I still have the phone numbers, the addresses
where I'll find the voices of dead men.
I live just off the back stairs,
in my temple throbs a bell
yanked out with the meat.
All night I wait for precious guests
shifting the shackles of door chains.

—*Translated from the Russian by John Glad*

(1930)

For the thundering glory of years to come,
For the valiant tribe of men,
I've relinquished the cup at the elders' repast
And my gaiety, honor and grace.

Our wolfhound age digs its teeth in my neck,
But I am no wolf in my blood,
Better stuff me away like a hat in the sleeve
Of the shaggy Siberian steppe.

So that I would see no coward or mud,
No bloody remains on the wheel,
So that, every night, foxes glowed for me,
Dazzling in the silver attire.

Take me into the night where the Yenisey flows
And the pine-trees reach out to the stars,
For, you know, I am no wolf in my blood,
Me — no one but an equal destroys.

—*Translated from the Russian by Maria Enzensberger*

(1931)

The day was rearing its five heads. For five
  long days and nights,
Shrinking, I was taking pride in the space
  that spread around like dough.
Sleep was older than hearing, hearing older than sleep —
  keen and solid.
Roads careered, chasing us
  in a coachman's race.
The day was rearing its five heads. Mad
  from the dance,
Mounted men went on riding,
  the black mass trudged along.
The expansion of power's aorta
  through white nights, no — knives —
Turned eyes into coniferous flesh.
If only I could have an inch of blue sea,
  just a needle's eye full...
To enable the escort of time to sail smoothly.
Russian fairy tale — humble meal. Wooden spoon.
  Haloo!
Where are you, the three lovely lads
  from the iron gate to the G P U?
To make sure Pushkin's marvelous goods
  did not pass into parasites' hands
A tribe of Pushkin scholars —
  in overcoats and with guns —
Is getting its schooling
  — Young lovers of whitetoothed rhymes
If only I could have an inch of blue sea,
  just a needle's eye full...
The train was speeding towards the Urals.
  Out of a sound movie,
Chapayev was riding into our open mouths
  to die
Behind a wooden stockade on a white sheet, die
  and jump onto his horse.

     —Translated from the Russian by Maria Enzensberger

(1935)

Charlie Chaplin
     Stepped out of the cinema,
Two soles,
    A harelip,
Two peepers
    Full of ink
And of fine astonished energy.
Charlie Chaplin —
    A harelip,
Two soles —
    A wretched fate.
Something is the matter with the way we all live.
      Strangers, strangers.
Pewter horror
    On his face,
The head
    Wouldn't hold up,
Soot is walking,
    Shoe polish is mincing,
And softly-softly
    Chaplin says:
What's the point
    Of my being cherished and loved,
      Even celebrated?
And a big highroad takes him to
      Strangers, strangers.
Charlie Chaplin,
    Press upon the pedal,
Charlie, rabbit,
    Break into your role,
Peel blood-oranges,
    Put on your roller-skates.
Your wife
    Is a blind shadow,
And the foreign land ahead ever unpredictable.
Why is it
    That Chaplin has a tulip?
Why
  Is the crowd so friendly?
Because this,
    After all, is Moscow.
Charlie, Charlie,
    You must take risks,

This is not time to get dispirited.
Your bowler hat
      Is but another ocean,
And Moscow is so close
            That one feels bewitched
            By the beckoning road.

—*Translated from the Russian by Maria Enzensberger*

(1937)

PERMISSIONS

"Insomnia," "On Stony Pierian Spurs," "I Am Deaf," and "Leningrad"
Reprinted from *Twentieth-Century Russian Poetry*, edited by John Glad and Daniel Weissbort (Iowa City: University of Iowa Press, 1992). Copyright ©1992 by the University of Iowa Press. Reprinted by permission of the University of Iowa Press.

["Can't remember how long"], ["For the thundering glory of years to come"] ["The day was rearing its five heads"], and ["Charlie Chaplin / stepped out"]
Reprinted from *A Necklace of Bees: Selected Poems*, trans. by Maria Enzensberger (London: The Menard Press/King's College London, 1992). Copyright ©1992 by the Estate of Maria Enzensberger. Reprinted by permission of The Menard Press.

João Cabral de Melo Neto [Brazil]
1920–1999

Born in Recife, Brazil in 1920, Melo Neto is the ac-
knowledged leader of the Brazilian poets of his gen-
eration. His early work was a reaction, in part, to the
intense verbal experimentation and the ethnocen-
trism of the early Brazilian modernists. Influenced
by Manuel Bandeira and Carlos Drummond de
Andrade, as well as by American and French writers
such as Marianne Moore and Paul Valéry, Melo Neto
worked toward a highly personal, vaguely surrealist
poetry. His first book, *Pedro do Sono*, was privately
published in Recife in 1942.

Following this book, however, he moved quickly
away from that poetic position, working toward a
new theory of poetic process. Over the next several
years, Melo Neto began to see poetry as a highly personal and self-conscious act, stressing the
formal, geometric aspects of his writing. Having moved to Rio de Janeiro in 1942, three years
later he joined the diplomatic serivce, and in 1945 was assigned to his first diplomatic post in
Barcelona, Spain. In 1950 he was sent to the Brazilian mission in London, and over the next
several years, served there until he was appointed the head of Brazil's Ministry of Agriculture in
1961. During these years some of Melo Neto's major works appeared, including *Psicologia da
composição* (Psychology of composition), *O cão sem plumas* (The dog without feathers), *O rio*
(The river), which won the Premio José Anchieta award for poetry, *Paisagens com figuras* (Land-
scapes with figures), *Morte e vida severina* ("Death and Life of a Severino"), and *Quaderna*
(Fourspot).

Morte e vida severina, in particular, marked a turn from the more intellectualized works of
form to issues of social consciousness, exemplied in this verse drama drawn from Northeastern
Brazilian folk traditions and stories. Melo Neto himself saw this as a synthesis, expressed in
"Education by Stone," whereby he worked to get the more elemental aspects of nature and
culture.

In the mid-1960s, Melo Neto returned to diplomatic service, spending periods of time in
Geneva, Barcelona, and Paraguay. He was appointed ambassador to Senegal in 1972, and began
as ambassador to Honduras in 1982. During this period he continued to write and publish new
books. He was elected to the Brazilian Academy of Letters in 1968. In 1988 he returned to Rio de
Janeiro. He was awarded the Camões Prize in 1991, the Neustadt International Prize for Litera-
ture in 1992, and the State of São Paulo Literary Prize the same year.

BOOKS OF POETRY:

Pedra do sono (Recife: privately printed, 1942); *Os três mal-amados* (published in *Revista do
Brazil*, 1943); *O engenheiro* (Rio de Janeiro: Amigos da Poesia, 1945); *Psicologia da composição,
com a fábula de Anfion e Antiode* (Barcelona: O Livro Inconsútil, 1947); *O cão sem plumas*
(Barcelona: O Livro Inconsútil, 1950); *Poemas reunidos* (Rio de Janeiro: Ordenou, 1954); *O rio
ou relação da viagem que faz o Capibaribe de sua nascente à cidade do Recife* (São Paulo: Comissão

do IV Centenário da Cidade de São Paulo, 1954); *Pregão turístico* (Recife: Aloísio Magelhães, 1955); *Duas águas* (Rio de Janeiro: José Olympio, 1956); *Aniki Bobó* (Recife: Aloísio Magalhães, 1958); *Quaderna* (Lisbon: Guimarães, 1960); *Dois parlamentos* (Madrid: Editôra do Autor, 1961); *Terceira feira* (Rio de Janeiro: Editôra do Autor, 1961); *Poemas escolhidos* (Lisbon: Portugália, 1963); *Antologia poética* (Rio de Janeiro: Editôra do Autor, 1963); *Morte e vida severina* (São Paulo: Teatro da Universidade Católica de São Paulo, 1965); *Morte e vida severina e outros poemas em voz alta* (Rio de Janeiro: Editôra do Autor, 1966); *A educação pela pedra* (Rio de Janeiro: Editôra do Autor, 1966); *Funeral de um lavrador* (São Paulo: Editôra Musical Arlequim, 1967); *Poesias completas (1940–1965)* (Rio de Janeiro: Sabiá, 1968); *Museu de tudo (1966–1974)* (Rio de Janeiro: José Olympio, 1975); *escola das facas* (Rio de Janeiro: José Olympio, 1980); *Poesia crítica* (Rio de Janeiro: José Olympio, 1982); *Auto do frade* (Nova Fronteira, 1984); *Argestes* (Rio de Janeiro: Nova Fronteira, 1985); *Os melhores poemas de João Cabral* (Rio de Janeiro: Global, 1985); *Crime na Calle Relator* (Rio de Janeiro: Nova Fronteira, 1987); *Museu de tudo e depois* (Rio de Janeiro: Nova Fronteira, 1988); *Poemas pernambucanos* (Rio de Janeiro: Nova Fronteira, 1988); *Sevilha andando* (Rio de Janeiro: Nova Fronteira, 1989); *Primeiros poemas* (Rio de Janeiro: Universidade Federal do Rio de Janeiro, 1990)

ENGLISH LANGUAGE TRANSLATIONS:

Selections in *Modern Brazilian Poetry*, ed. by John Nist (Bloomington: Indiana University Press, 1962); *The Rebounding Stone*, trans. by A.B.M. Cadaxa (London: Outposts, 1967); selections in *An Anthology of Twentieth Century Brazilian Poetry*, ed. by Elizabeth Bishop (Middletown, Connecticut: Wesleyan University Press [University Press of New England], 1972); *Selected Poetry 1937–1990*, ed. by Djelal Kadir (Hanover, New Hampshire: Wesleyan University Press [University Press of New England], 1994).

Pirandello II

I know there are millions of men
mixing themselves up this moment.
The director took hold of all consciousnesses
and keeps them in this bag of hornets.
Then he multiplied them
not quite as bread was multiplied
by ten, by forty thousand.
His gesture was as if distributing flowers.
A monk, a pianist, a wagon driver was my lot.
I was a failed artist
who had exhausted all the backstages
I felt as tired as the horses
of those who are not heroes
I will be a monk
a wagon driver and a pianist
and I shall have to hang myself three times.

—Translated from the Portuguese by Richardo da Silveira Lobo Sternberg

Daily Space

In the daily space
the shadow eats the orange
the orange throws itself into the river,
it's not a river, it's the sea
overflowing from my eye.

In the daily space
born out of the clock
I see hands not words,
late at night I dream up the woman,
I have the woman and the fish.

In the daily space
I forget the home the sea
I lose hunger memory
I kill myself uselessly
in the daily space.

—Translated from the Portuguese by W. S. Merwin

(*Pedra do sono*, 1942)

Within the Loss of Memory

To José Guimarães de Araújo

Within the loss of memory
a blue woman reclined
hiding in her arms one
of those cold birds
that the moon floats late at night
on the naked shoulders of the portrait.

And from the portrait two flowers grew
(two eyes two breasts two clarinets)
that at certain hours of the day
grew prodigiously
so that the bicycles of my desperation
might run over her hair.

And on the bicycles that were poems
my hallucinated friends arrived.
Seated in apparent disorder
swallowing their watches with regularity
while the hierophant armed as horseman
uselessly moved his lone arm.

—Translated from the Portuguese by Djelal Kadir

(*Pedra do sono*, 1942)

I
(Landscape of the Capibaribe River)

§ The city is crossed by the river
as a street
is crossed by a dog,
a piece of fruit
by a sword.

§ The river called to mind
a dog's docile tongue,
or a dog's sad belly,
or that other river
which is the dirty wet cloth
of a dog's two eyes.

§ The river was
like a dog without feathers.
It knew nothing of the blue rain,
of the rose-colored fountain,
of the water in a water glass,
of the water in pitchers,
of the fish in the water,
of the breeze on the water.

§ It knew the crabs
of mud and rust.
It knew silt
like a mucous membrane.
It must have known the octopus,
and surely knew
the feverish woman living in oysters.

§ The river
never opens up to fish,
to the shimmer,
to the knifely unrest
existing in fish.
It never opens up in fish.

§ It opens up in flowers,
poor and black
like black men and women.
It opens up into a flora
as squalid and beggarly
as the blacks who must beg.
It opens up in hard-leafed
mangroves, kinky
as a black man's hair.

§ Smooth like the belly
of a pregnant dog,
the river swells
without ever bursting.
The river's childbirth
is like a dog's,
fluid and invertebrate.

§ And I never saw it seethe
   (as bread when rising
   seethes).
   In silence
   the river bears its bloating poverty,
   pregnant with black earth.

§ It yields in silence:
   in black earthen capes,
   in black earthen boots or gloves
   for the foot or hand
   that plunges in.

§ As sometimes happens
   with dogs, the river
   seemed to stagnate.
   Its waters would turn
   thicker and warmer,
   flowing with the thick
   warm waves
   of a snake.

§ It had something
   of a crazy man's stagnation.
   Something of the stagnation
   of hospitals, prisons, asylums,
   of the dirty and smothered life
   (dirty, smothering laundry)
   it trudged through.

§ Something of the stagnation
   of decayed palaces,
   eaten
   by mold and mistletoe.
   Something of the stagnation
   of obese trees
   dripping a thousand sugars
   from the Pernambuco dining rooms
   it trudged through.

§ (It is there,
with their backs to the river,
that the city's "cultured families"
brood over the fat eggs
of their prose.
In the complete peace of their kitchens
they viciously stir
their pots
of sticky indolence.)

§ Could the river's water
be the fruit of some tree?
Why did it seem
like ripened water?
Why the flies always
above it, as if about to land?

§ Did any part of the river
ever cascade in joy?
Was it ever, anywhere,
a song or fountain?
Why then
were its eyes painted blue
on maps?

—*Translated from the Portuguese by Richard Zenith*

(*O cão sem plumas*, 1950)

Written with the Body

Such is her composition
and articulate syntax
that she is apprehended
only in the sum, never in parts.

There is no single term
where attention is arrested;
or that, however significant,
exclusively holds her key.

Nor can she be parsed
like a sentence; impossible
to derive a paraphrase
from what in her is sense.

And just as, only complete
is she capable of revelation,
only another body, complete,
has the faculty to apprehend her.

Only a body in its completeness
undivided by analysis
can engage in the *corps a corps*
needed by whomever, not reducing,

wants to capture all the themes
inscribed in that body-phrase
that she, composure intact,
reveals with such intensity.

§

Seen from afar, like a Mondrian
reproduced in a magazine,
she betrays only the indifferent
perfection of geometry.

Up close, however, the original,
seen before as cold correctness,
free of the interfering camera
of distance and its lenses;

up close, however, the close eye
free of extraneous retinas;
up close, when sight is tactile;
to the quick and naked eye

one can discern in her
an unsuspected energy
revealed by the Mondrian
when seen in the canvas.

Yet in one respect
she differs from a Mondrian:
what in her is vibrant
and goes unnoticed from afar

can forego the flame of colors
without which a Mondrian is static,
can vibrate with the white texture
of wholesome skin, or canvas.

When he is dressed with only
her smooth nakedness
he feels more than undressed:
feels more completely so.

§

He is, in fact, undressed
save for the clothes which she is
but these he does not wear:
internal ones slip off.

When the body dresses itself
with she-clothes, with she-silk
it feels itself more defined
than it does when wearing clothes.

It feels itself more than undressed
for its secret skin
soon unravels and it assumes
her skin, which she lets him borrow.

But the borrowed skin also
does not last long as clothes
for very easily she too
unravels and is divested

until she's left with nothing,
neither skin, nor silk:
all is mingled, common
nakedness, without boundaries.

§

She is, when she is not here,
held by an outside memory.
Outside: as if she were held
by an external type of memory.

A memory for the body,
external to it, like a purse.
Like a purse, certain gestures
cause it to touch the body.

A memory external to the body
not the one growing inside;
and that, since intended for the body,
carries corporeal presences.

So it is within this memory
that she, unexpectedly, is embodied
in the presence, thingness, volume
of a body, solidly there

and that is now dense volume
in the arms and held by them,
and that is now hollow volume
that surrounds and shelters the body

as something that was both dense
and hollow at the same time
that the body had, where it was
as if the having and the being were one.

> —*Translated from the Portuguese*
> *by Ricardo da Silveira Lobo Sternberg*

(*Serial,* collected in *Terceira feira,* 1961)

Education by Stone

An education by stone: through lessons,
to learn from the stone: to go to it often,
to catch its level, impersonal voice
(by its choice of words it begins its classes).
The lesson in morals, the stone's cold resistance
to flow, to flowing, to being hammered:
the lesson in poetics, its concrete flesh:
in economics, how to grow dense compactly:
lessons from the stone, (from without to within,
dumb primer), for the routine speller of spells.

Another education by stone: in the backlands
(from within to without and pre-didactic place).
In the backlands stone does not know how to lecture,
and, even if it did would teach nothing:
you don't learn the stone, there: there, the stone,
born stone, penetrates the soul.

—*Translated from the Portuguese by James Wright*

(*A educação pela pedra*, 1966)

PERMISSIONS

"Pirandello II," "Daily Space," "Within the Loss of Memory," "Landscape of the Capibaribe River," and "Education by Stone"
Reprinted from *Selected Poetry, 1937–1990*, edited by Djelal Kadir and trans. by Ricardo da Silveira Lobo Sternberg, W. S. Merwin, Djelal Kadir, Richard Zenith, and James Wright (Hanover, New Hampshire: Wesleyan University Press [University Press of New England], 1994). Copyright ©1994 by Wesleyan University Press. Reprinted by permission of the University Press of New England.

Henri Michaux [Belgium]
1899–1984

Henri Michaux was born in Namur, Belgium in 1899 to a middle-class family. From early childhood, Michaux demonstrated some of the tendencies which were to define his entire life: food disgusted him, and he shunned games, amusements, and other children. He also suffered from anemia. Also in those early years, as throughout his life, he became interested and terrified by his dreams, particularly his dreams without images or words, what he called "motionless" dreams.

In 1906 his was sent to the country, to a little village in Campine near Holland. His classes were in Flemish and his classmates were the sons of poor peasants. He remained secretive, withdrawn, and, mostly, ashamed—ashamed of being who he was and ashamed of everything around him.

At age 12 he moved to Brussels, attending a Jesuit school. But here he felt more at home, and discovered the pleasures of the dictionary. With his father's prodding, he became interested in Latin and in music. The five years of German Occupation in World War I, however, continued to isolate him, and he retreated into a world of reading: bizarre writers, the lives of saints and mystics such as Ernest Hello and Ruysbroek.

In 1919 he attended medical school, but did not show up for the final exams, and abandoned a medical career. The following year, Michaux shipped out as a sailor on a schooner, beginning the travels which would continue throughout his life. Throughout 1920 and into 1921, he traveled the world, visiting the ports of Bremen, Savannah, Norfolk, Newport News, Rio de Janeiro, Buenos Aires, New York. His return to Brussels in 1922 brought on a new sense of despair and disgust, and at the end of that year he moved to Paris, where he began writing.

Michaux's writings and art are all set against literary and artistic stereotypes, as he sought in his work a visionary focus which followed the inner movements of the unconscious and, at times, hallucinatory world. His first book, *Qui je fus* (Who I Was) is just such a work in which Michaux explored enigmas and apparent contradictions in his own life. *Mes propriétés* of 1929 is, in many ways, a precursor of Beckett in its presentation of alienated man, its absurd humor and its struggle with the psychologies of its characters (presented in both poetry and prose).

In the same year, Michaux traveled to Ecuador, recounting in his book of that title his journey from the Andes to the Amazon. The result was an often-times abrasive and unillusioned presentation of what romantics and exoticists had expressed before him. *Un Barbare en Asie (A Barbarian in Asia)*, is, on the other hand, a joyful and rhapsodic recounting of his encounters with the various Indians, Malays, Chinese, Indonesians, and Japanese of his voyage.

In 1938 Gallimard published his *Plume, précédé de Lointain intérieur,* continuing the adventures of his comic, absurdist hero, Plume, who awakens in a room without walls, dines on food not on the menu, and travels—despite being thrown *off* a train and *into* the ship's hold—feeling fortunate for his ability to do so.

During World War II, he and his wife suffered from the shortages of food which he had once found so disgusting. His wife contracted tuberculosis, and throughout the next couple of years, they traveled to Egypt and elsewhere in hopes of a cure. Then, in 1948, his wife died suddenly "as a result of atrocious burns."

Perhaps his masterwork is *Ailleurs* (1948), written the same year. It is a work described by the author as "buffer-states" situated between external observation and interest obsession. This trilogy is reminiscent of the works of Swift, Huxley, and other dystopian works.

In the early 1950s, Michaux withdrew for a while from writing, spending more time on his painting. But in 1954, he published one of his major works, *Face aux verrous* (Facing the Locks), which contained a long prose poem on the death of his wife and several works that, in their hallucinatory quality, foretell of his later experimentation with drugs. He died at the age of 85.

BOOKS OF POETRY:

Qui je fus (Paris: Gallimard, 1927); *Mes propriétés* (Paris: Fourcade, 1929); *Un Certain Plume* (Paris: Carrefour, 1930); *La Nuit remue* (Paris: Gallimard, 1935; revised, 1967); *Plume, précédé de Lointain intérieur* (Paris: Gallimard, 1938; revised, 1977); *Au pays de la magie* (Paris: Gallimard, 1941; revised, 1977); *Épreuves, exorcismes 1940-44* (Paris: Gallimard, 1945); *Liberté d'Action* (Paris: Fontaine, 1945); *Apparitions* (Paris: Point du Jour, 1946); *Ici Poddema* (Lausanne: Mermod, 1946); *Ailleurs* (Paris: Gallimard, 1948; revised, 1967); *La Vie dans les plis* (Paris: Gallimard, 1949); *Poésie pour pouvoir* (Paris: Drouin, 1949); *Passages 1937–1950* (Paris: Gallimard, 1950; revised, 1963); *Mouvements* (Paris: Gallimard, 1952); *Face aux verrous* (Paris: Gallimard, 1954; revised, 1967); *Paix dans les brisements* (Paris: Flinker, 1959); *Vers la complétude (Saisie et dessaisies)* (Paris: GLM, 1967); *Moments: Traversées du temps* (Paris: Gallimard, 1973); *Choix de poèmes* (Paris: Gallimard, 1976); *Chemins cherchés, Chemains perdus, Transgressions* (Paris: Gallimard, 1981); *Déplacements dégagements* (Paris: Gallimard, 1985).

ENGLISH LANGUAGE TRANSLATIONS:

The Space Within: Selected Writings, 1927-1959 (New York: New Directions, 1951); *Henri Michaux: Selections,* trans. by Teo Savory (Santa Barbara, California: Unicorn Press, 1967); *The Selected Writings of Henri Michaux,* trans. by Richard Ellmann (New York: New Directions, 1968); *Darkness Moves: An Henri Michaux Anthology, 1927-1984,* trans. by David Ball (Berkeley: University of California Press, 1994).

The Big Fight

He grabowerates him and grabacks him to the ground;
He rads him and rabarts him to his drat;
He braddles him and lippucks him and prooks his bawdles;
He tackreds him and marmeens him
Mandles him rasp by rip and risp by rap.
And he deskinnibilizes him at the end.

The other hesitates; he is bittucked, unapsed, torsed and ruined.
He'll be done for soon.
He mendles and marginates himself...but in vain,
The far-rolling hoop falls down.
Abrah! Abrah! Abrah!
The foot has failed!
The arm has broke!
The blood has flowed!
Gouge, gouge, gouge,
In the big pot of his belly there's a great secret
You hags all around us crying into your handkerchiefs,
We're amazed, amazed, amazed
We're watching you
We're looking for the Great Secret, too.

—*Translated from the French by David Ball*

(from *Qui je fus*, 1927)

Insects

As I went farther west, I saw nine-segmented insects with huge eyes like graters and latticework corselets like miners' lamps, others with murmuring antennae; some with twenty-odd pairs of legs that looked more like staples; others of black lacquer and mother-of-pearl that crunched underfoot like shells; still others high legged like daddy longlegs with little pin-eyes as red as the eyes of albino mice, veritable glowing coals on stems with an expression of ineffable panic; still others with an ivory head—surprisingly bald, so that suddenly one had the most fraternal feelings for them—so close, their legs kicking forward like piston rods zigzagging in the air.

Finally, there were transparent ones, bottles with hairy spots, perhaps: they came forward by the thousands—glassware, a display of light and sun so bright that afterward everything seemed ash and product of dark night.

—*Translated from the French by David Ball*

(from *Mes propriétés*, 1929)

Under the Obsessive Beacon of Fear

It's still only a small halo, nobody sees it, but *he* knows that out of it will come the fire, a tremendous fire will come, and him smack in the middle of it, he's going to have to adjust, to keep on living as before (How you doing? O.K., and yourself?), ravaged by the conscientious devouring fire.

*

(...)

*

...and fear makes no exceptions.

When a deep-sea fish goes mad and swims anxiously over to the fish in its family at a depth of two thousand feet—bumps into them, wakes them up, accosting them one after the other:

"Don't *you* hear the sound of running water?"

"You don't hear a thing down there?"

"Don't you hear something going 'cheh,' no, softer: 'chee, chee'?"

"Watch out, don't move, we'll hear it again."

Oh, Fear, you terrible Master!

The wolf is afraid of the violin. The elephant is afraid of mice, pigs, firecrackers. And the agouti shudders in its sleep.

—*Translated from the French by David Ball*

(from *La Nuit remue,* 1935)

The Village of Madmen

Once so lively, now a deserted village. Huddled under an open shed, a man was waiting for the rain to end; now, it was freezing cold, there would be no chance of rain for a long time to come.

A farmer was looking for his horse among the eggs. It had just been stolen. It was a market day. Countless were the eggs in countless baskets. Surely the thief had thought of this to discourage pursuit.

In a room of the white house, a man was dragging his wife toward the bed.

"Do you mind!" she said. "What if I were your father!"

"You can't be my father," he said, "since you're a woman, and besides, no man has two fathers."

"See, you're worried, too."

He left, disheartened; a Gentleman in evening dress passed by him and said:
"There are no more queens nowadays. There's no point going on about it, there *are*
no more." And he walked away, muttering threats.

—Translated from the French by David Ball

(from *La Nuit remue*, 1935)

In the Night

In the night
In the night
I have united with the night
With the endless night
With the night.
Mine, queen, queen of mine.
Night
Night of birth
Filling me with my cry
My flowering spikes.
You, invading me
with howl howl swells
all over ocean swells
smoking dense
and bellowing,
are the night.
Here lies the night, relentless night.
And its brass band, and its beach,
Its beach above, its beach all over,
Its beach drinking, with its weight king, sinking things beneath,
Beneath it, beneath thinner than a thread
Beneath the night
The Night.

—Translated from the French by David Ball

(from *Plume, précédé de Lointain intérieur,* 1938)

from A Certain Plume

II. Plume at the Restaurant

Plume was having lunch at the restaurant when the headwaiter came over, looked at him severely and said to him in a low, mysterious voice: "What you have on your plate is *not* on the menu."

Plume apologized immediately.

"Well sir," he said, "since I was in a hurry, I didn't bother reading the menu. I ordered a chop, just like that, thinking that perhaps you had one, or if you didn't, that you could easily find one nearby, but I was ready to order something quite different if there were no chops around. The waiter didn't seem particularly surprised, he went away and brought it in a bit later and so...

Naturally I'll pay the price for it, whatever it may be. It's a nice cut of meat, I won't deny it. I'll pay the price without hesitation. If I had known, I would gladly have chosen another kind of meat or simply an egg—and anyway I'm not very hungry any more. I'll pay you right away."

But the headwaiter does not move. Plume is terribly embarrassed. After a while, when he looks up... Uh-oh! Now the manager is standing there in front of him.

Plume apologizes immediately.

"I did not realize," he says, "that chops weren't on the menu. I didn't look at it, because I have extremely bad eyesight, and I didn't have my pince-nez on me, and besides, reading always gives me a terrible pain. I asked for the first thing that came into my mind and more to elicit other suggestions than out of personal taste. The waiter, who no doubt had other things on his mind, didn't think twice about it, he brought me this, and as for me, I'm quite absentminded and I began to eat, so...I'll pay you personally as long as you're here."

But the manager doesn't move. Plume feels more and more embarrassed. As he is holding a bill out to him, he suddenly sees the sleeve of a uniform; it's a policeman standing in front of him.

Plume apologizes immediately.

Well sir, he had come in to rest a bit. Suddenly, they shouted at him point-blank, "And for Monsieur? You would like...?" "Oh, a glass of beer." "And then what..." the angry waiter had shouted; so, more to get rid of him than for any other reason, Plume had said: "O.K., a chop!"

He was no longer thinking about it by the time it was brought in on a plate; then, well, since there it was right in front of him...

"Listen, if you would try to settle this business, it would be very nice of you. Here's something for you."

And he holds out a hundred franc bill. As he hears receding footsteps, he thinks he's home free. But now it's the police commissioner standing there.

Plume apologizes immediately.

He had an appointment with a friend. He had looked for him in vain all morning. So, since he knew that his friend walked by this street on his way home from the office, he had come in here, had taken a table near the window and moreover, since there might be a long wait and he didn't want to look as if he were reluctant to spend money, he had ordered a chop—just to have something in front of him. Not for a moment did he think of eating it. But since he had it in front of him, mechanically, without having the slightest idea of what he was doing, he had begun to eat.

They should realize that he wouldn't go to a restaurant for anything on earth. He always has lunch at home. It's one of his principles. This was a case of pure absent-mindedness, the kind of thing that can happen to anyone when he's upset—a moment of thoughtlessness, no more than that.

But the commissioner has phoned the head of the criminal division: "Come on," he says to Plume as he hands him the phone. "Explain yourself once and for all. It's your only chance." And a policeman, shoving him roughly, says to him: "From now on you've got to walk the straight and narrow, got it?" And as firemen are pouring into the restaurant, the manager says to him: "Look what a loss I'm going to take. A real disaster!" And he points to the dining room: all the customers have rushed out.

The men from the Secret Police are telling him: "It's going to get rough, we're warning you. You'd better confess everything, the whole truth. This isn't the first job we've handled, believe you me. When it starts going this way, it's really serious."

Meanwhile, a huge, tough cop over his shoulder is saying to him: "Listen, I can't do anything about it. I've got orders. If you don't talk into the phone, I start hitting. Get it? Confess! I'm warning you. If I don't hear you, I start hitting."

—*Translated from the French by David Ball*

(from *Plume, précédé de Lointain intérieur*, 1938)

On the Spit

A sling for some, a spit for others...and it's so natural. Hard to keep your chair. The guests are eating. You have to make room. New ones are coming in. Where to put the earlier ones. Where to put them? You put them on the spit.

Driven from chair to chair, from spot to spot, they find themselves in front of the fireplace. You push them in and *there!* on to the spit!

There's no lack of naturalness here. Nothing to complain about, as far as naturalness is concerned.

That's why no one resists. Sucked in gently, but irresistibly, they slip toward the warm opening. The idea of resisting does not really come into their minds. They don't fight back, they have been struck by the obvious.

—*Translated from the French by David Ball*

(from *La Vie dans les plis*, 1949)

from Poetry for Power

1. I Am Rowing

I have cursed your forehead your belly your life
I have cursed the streets your steps plod through
The things your hands pick up
I have cursed the inside of your dreams

I have set a puddle in your eye that can't see any more
An insect in your ear that can't hear any more
A sponge in your brain that can't understand any more

I have frozen you in the soul of your body
Iced you in the depths of your life
The air you breathe suffocates you
The air you breathe has the air of a cellar
Is an air that has already been exhaled
been puffed out by hyenas
The dung of this air is something no one can breathe

Your skin is damp all over
Your skin sweats out waters of the great fear
Your armpits reek far and wide of the crypt

Animals stop dead as you pass
Dogs howl at night, their heads raised toward your house
You can't run away
You can't muster the strength of an ant to the tip of your feet
Your fatigue makes a lead stump in your body
Your fatigue is a long caravan
Your fatigue stretches out to the country of Nan
Your fatigue is inexpressible

Your mouth bites you
Your nails scratch you
No longer yours, your wife
No longer yours, your brother
The sole of his foot bitten by an angry snake

Someone has slobbered on your descendants
Someone has slobbered on the laugh of your little girl
Someone has walked slobbering by the face of your domain

The world moves away from you

I am rowing
I am rowing
I am rowing against your life
I am rowing
I split into countless rowers
To row more strongly against you

You fall into blurriness
You are out of breath
You get tired before the slightest effort

I row
I row
I row

You go off drunk, tied to the tail of a mule
Drunkenness like a huge umbrella that darkens the sky
And assembles the flies
Dizzy drunkenness of the semicircular canals
Unnoticed beginnings of hemiplegia
Drunkenness no longer leaves you
Lays you out to the left
Lays you out to the right
Lays you out on the stony ground of the path
I row
I row
I am rowing against your days

You enter the house of suffering

I row
I row
On a black blindfold your actions are recorded
On the great white eye of a one-eyed horse your future is rolling

I AM ROWING

—Translated from the French by David Ball

(from *Face aux verrous*, 1954)

The Days, the Days, the End of Days

Meditation on the end of Paul Celan.

. . . .
In silence, stoned to death by their thoughts

Still another day on a lesser level. Shadowless gestures
What century must we look at, to see?

Ferns, ferns, they might be sighs, everywhere, sighs
The wind scatters the loose leaves

Strength of stretchers, eighteen hundred thousand years ago people
were already born to rot, to die, to suffer

We've already had days like this
so many days like this

day that swallows up the wind
day of unbearable thoughts

I see men motionless
lying in barges

Out of here.
Whatever else, out of here.

The long knife of the wave will stop the Word.

—Translated from the French by David Ball

(from *Moments: Traversées du temps,* 1973)

O.[scar] V.[ladislas] de L.[ubicz] Milosz [Lithuania / France] 1877–1939

Milosz was born in Lithuania in 1877. The country home of his parents and the surrounding landscape of dark forests and decaying châteaux were to have an influence on his writing for the rest of his life. At the age of twelve, his parents sent him to Paris, where he was educated in European languages as well as in Greek, Latin, and Hebrew.

His youth was spent in travel, experiences from which he used throughout his writing. His first poems, published in 1899, were collected in *Le Poème des Décadences,* written out of his experiences as a member of the Paris circle of writers and artists who frequented the Closerie des Lilas. Milosz continued to frequent that café for the rest of his life, long after it had lost its special status and had become a place for tourists.

For ten years after World War I, Milosz was minister-resident for Lithuania, and wrote several historical and political treatises on the problems of his home country and the Baltic States. He also gathered three collections of Lithuanian folklore. But in 1930, he became a French citizen. He died on March 2, 1939, the eve of World War II.

His poetry is filled with the sense of Paris and pre-World War II Parisian life, sensual, and dark, clearly influenced by the writings of Baudelaire and Gautier. Milosz was also a scholar, and wrote metaphysical tracts and dramas.

BOOKS OF POETRY:

Le Poème des Décadences (Paris: Girard et Villerelle, 1899); *Les Sept Solitudes* (Paris: Henry Jouve, 1906); *Les Éléments* (Paris: Bibliothèque de L'Occident, 1911); *Poèmes* (Paris: Éditions Figuière, 1915); *Adramandoni* (Paris: M. Duncan, 1918); *La Confession de Lemuel* (Paris: La Connaissance, 1922); *Poèmes: 1895–1927* (Paris: J. O. Fourcade, 1929); *Dix-sept Poëmes de Milosz* (Tunis: Éditions de Mirages, 1937); *Poèmes* (Paris: Cahiers des Poètes Catholiques, 1938).

ENGLISH LANGUAGE TRANSLATIONS:

Fourteen Poems, trans. by Kenneth Rexroth (Port Townsend, Washington: Copper Canyon Press, 1983); *The Noble Traveller,* edited by Christopher Bamford (Hudson, New York: Lindisfarne Press, 1985).

When she comes...

When she comes—will her eyes be grey or green,
Green or grey on the river?
The hour will be new in a future so old,
New, but not very new...
Old hours where everything has been said, everything seen, everything dreamed!
I pity you if you know it.

There will be today and the city noises,
Just like today and every day—hard problems!—
And smells—depending on the season—of September or April
And a false sky and some clouds in the river;

And some words—depending on the moment—gay or sobbing
Under skies that rejoice or weep,
For we will have lived and feigned so much again and again,
When she comes with her eyes like a rainy river.

There will be (voice of weariness, laughter of impotence)
The senile, the sterile, the dry present moment,
The throbbing of eternity, sister of silence,
The present moment, just like the present.

Yesterday, ten years ago, today, a month from now,
Horrible words, dead thoughts, which mean nothing,
Drink, sleep, die,—we must escape from ourselves
In one way or another...

—Translated from the French by Kenneth Rexroth

(from *Les Sept Solitudes*, 1906)

Monkey Dance

To the tune of a little mocking music, frisking
Breathlessly, and weeping, weeping like the pouring rain,
Jump, jump, my soul, old monkey, to the Barbary organ,
Little old ragamuffin, sly, romantic and tender animal.

With your tail like leafless autumn, pretentiously twisted
In a question mark against the empty twilight sky,

Wipe your tears, gallant monkey, melancholy and ridiculous,
Monkey scabby with dead love, monkey toothless with lost days.

Another tune, give us another tune! You know the low dives,
The leprous slums, the autumn street fairs, the sour fish and chips.
You make the malnourished girls laugh,—o dirty, frightful, skinny,
Piteous, epileptic monkey, animal of pure homesickness.

Give us another tune, too bad it's the last!—And let it be that sordid
Last waltz, the requiem of dead thieves, echoing music
Which says, "Goodbye memory, love and coconuts..."
While the poor rain gurgles in the old and heavy mud.

—Translated from the French by Kenneth Rexroth

(from *Les Sept Solitudes*, 1906)

November Symphony

It will be exactly like this life. The same room.
Yes, my child, the same. At dawn the bird of time in the foliage
Pale as a corpse. Then the servants will get up,
And you will hear the frozen noises, in the hollow basins

Of the fountains. O terrible, terrible youth! O empty heart!
It will be exactly like this life. There will be
The poor voices, the voices of winter in old slums,
The glass mender singing his own duet,

The broken grandmother under a dirty bonnet
Crying out the names of fish, the man with the blue apron
Who spits into a hand worn by the wheelbarrow
And yells nobody knows what, like the Angel of Judgment.

It will be exactly like this life. The same table.
The Bible, Goethe, the ink and the smell of time,
The paper, white woman who reads thoughts,
The pen, the portrait. My child, my child!

It will be exactly like this life!—The same garden,
Deep, deep, thick, dim. And towards noon

People will enjoy themselves at being reunited there
Who never met and who do not know

One from another. You will have to dress
As if for a party and go in the night
Of the lost, all alone, without love and without lamp.
It will be exactly like this life. The same parkway:

And (in the autumn afternoon), at the turn of the parkway,
There where the beautiful road goes down shyly, like the woman
Who goes to pick the flowers of convalescence—listen, my child,
We shall meet again, here as of old,

And you have forgotten, the color your dress was then,
But I, I have known only little moments of happiness.
You will be garbed in pale violet, beautiful sorrow!
And the flowers of your hat will be small and sad,

And I will not know their names, for in this life I have known
Only the name of one sad small flower, the forget-me-not,
The old sleeper in the ravines of the land of hide and seek,
The orphan flower. Yes, yes, deep heart, like this life.

And the dim path will be there, all damp
In the echo of waterfalls. And I will tell you
About the city upon the water, and about Rabbi Bacharach,
And about the nights of Florence. There will also be

The sinking wall and down there where the smells
Of the old, old rain and the leprous weeds drowse,
Cold and fat, the hollow flowers shake there
In the dumb stream.

—*Translated from the French by Kenneth Rexroth*

(from *Poèmes*, 1915)

Psalm of the King of Beauty

From the Isles of Separation and the Empire of the Depths, hear the rising voice of the harps of the suns. Peace flows over our heads. The place where we now stand, Malchut, is the heart of Height.

The fruitful tears pour forth as I think of my Father and the worlds of gold shed a light of beauty on the depths. Royal head yet resting on my heart, what a fear of numbers you decipher in the memory of night! Queen, be truly a woman in supreme compassion. All white with pity for greatness, think of the Creator, most abandoned of all. The spot where we now stand, Malchut, is the heart of Height.

Facing the saintly toil of the constellations, can you not feel your heart torn asunder, Malchut, Malchut, wife, mother too of generations? Space, a swarm of sacred bees, flies towards the Adramand of ecstatic perfumes. The spot where we now stand, Malchut, is the heart of Height.

For the motionless Absolute is the secret desire of that which moves. A solar regent and pious Sower of seed destined to be born and die, I love only what is permanent. I myself, I who am but a small personification, I desire ardently to become transmuted. Here in the abyss, nothing is situated, nothing is situated! All reality exists only in the love of the Father. The place where we now stand, Malchut, is the heart of Height.

Peace on earth, oh my spouse, oh woman! Peace in all the unreal empire, peace for the gentle souls for which you make the seven strings of the rainbow sing! When I contemplate, oh Queen, your overturned face, I have the deep feeling that all my thoughts are born in your sweet heart. The place where we now stand, Malchut, is the heart of Height.

And yet, and yet I would wish to fall asleep on this throne of Time and to fall from the depths to the heights in the divine abyss! To be seated forever motionless among the sages. To forget that the word HERE was lacking in my language. For I, who constantly create in order to deserve the Nothing, I am the desire of the end, Malchut, of the end and of the end of all ends. Oh, to retire to rest, dead spouse, in my heart, and then to be reborn for the Father's eternal day! The place where we now stand, Malchut, is the heart of Height.

—*Translated from the French by Edouard Roditi*

(from *Poèmes: 1895–1927*, 1929)

Psalm of the Morning Star

The torrents of flocks		pour down towards
the sheepfolds		shade covers An-Dor and
Pau of the land of Esau		covers Matred Toled Beith
Aram	and all Spared of Judea	Starred
memory	Israel's night of the soul	space
projected by lambs' eyes		Down yonder Artizarra
is already shining		on the brow of our Mother Iberia

her   Schourien-Ieschouroun   withdraws
hiding his face   beneath the sackcloth of the fog
Selah   Enough of your bleating at the sky
salted with white specks   let us go now my wall-lickers
to the salt of the wall of accustomed tearson the
hyssop pathway   between the butter hedgerows   pass
lambs of the king beneath the shepherd's crook   of iron
White nineteen black forth   and
thou forty-fourth   numbers traced by a
herdsman's hand   formed like little sticks   on some
wall of Beith lehem   they are more numerous than are
you up there   goat-kids of the Living one
of the betrothed sister of the new canticle
Selah   The hand   of the cedars of
benediction   is still as slow   upon our heads
arisen from the depths of the ages   in the language of
the Western sea   in vain does Naphschi try to
intercept   a single new word   the same
heart as in the time of the fathers   beats in wood
stone and water   of all that returns there is
nothing new   all those things were sleeping
in closed books   the books have opened themselves
beneath my hand   pass my beauties Judith
pass   good girls   under the iron
crook   Kimah Ksil and you the Mazaroths
and you the other skies   nameless innumerable
suspended aloft so high   in the great
hazes of God   holy old men cast down
towards the earth   your gazes of lost and
fractured flint   Aleleth-hascahar the shepherdess
comes down towards Guinath Agoz   the light's
jug of milk on her shoulder   she calls to the child Olel
guardian of the lions' pasture   caressed in
his sleep by vipers   Selah   Here things
are what they are   the eyelashes' steam
fires of rain at the roof-edge   in the
sower's sack handful of stars   and thy wheels
entering one into the other
Iehezkeel the terrible spirals   behold how here
things are what they are   deep profoundly deep
is That   he who bows down low
will be bowed down to

—*Translated from the French by David Gascoyne*

(from *Dix-Sept Poèmes de Milosz*, 1937)

Ágnes Nemes Nagy [Hungary]
1922–1991

Born in Budapest to a family with Transylvanian ties, Ágnes Nemes Nagy studied Hungarian and Latin at the University of Budapest, but her "intellectual birth," as she puts it, took place at a Calvinist gymnasium for girls with the renowned poet, Lajor Áprily, at its head.

She began her career as an editor for the postwar literary review *Újhold* (New Moon), which was banned in 1948. Her first book, *Kettös világban* (In a Dual World) was published and welcomed by the reviewers in 1946. A victim of the "szilencium," she could not publish again for nearly ten years. From 1953 to 1958 she taught in a secondary school. It was only in 1957, with the publication of *Száravillám* (Heat Lightning), that she came to the forefront of Hungarian poetry. After the publication of this book, she began to support herself from her own writing and translating works from German, French, and English.

Her third book of poems, *Napforduló* (Solstice), appeared in 1967, and brought her international attention. Other books followed, and in 1969 and 1981 she published collected works of her poetry, the first titled *A lovogok és az angyalok* (The Horses and the Angels), the second titled *Között* (Between). With her husband, the critic Baláczs Lengyle, she spent several months at the University of Iowa on a Writers' Visiting Fellowship. In 1983 she was awarded the prestigious Kossuth Prize. By the time of her death in 1991, she was recognized as one of Hungary's leading poets. She also wrote essays and poetry for children.

Nemes Nagy described herself as an "objective lyric poet," attracted to both objects and the objectivity of the lyric tone.

BOOKS OF POETRY:

Kettös világban (Budapest, 1946); *Szárazvillám* (Budapest, 1957); *Napforduló* (Budapest, 1967); *A Lovagok es az angyalok* (Budapest: Magvető Köngkiadó, 1969); *Között* (Budapest: Magvető Kiadó, 1981).

ENGLISH LANGUAGE TRANSLATIONS:

Selected Poems, trans. by Bruce Berlind (Iowa City: University of Iowa, 1980); *Between: Selected Poems of Ágnes Nemes Nagy*, trans. by Hugh Maxton (Budapest: Corvina, 1989); Selections in *The Colonnade of Teeth: Modern Hungarian Poetry*, edited by George Gömöri and George Szirtes (Newcastle upon Tyne: Bloodaxe Books, 1996).

To a Poet

My contemporary. He died, not I.
He fell near Tobruk, poor boy.
He was English. Other names, for us,
tell the places where, like ripe nuts,
heads fell and cracked in twos,
those portable radios,
their poise of parts and volume
finer than the Eiffel, lovely spinal column
as it crashed down to the earth.
That's how I think of your youth —
like a dotard who doesn't know
now from fifty years ago,
his heart in twilight, addlepated.

But love is complicated.

—Translated from the Hungarian by Bruce Berlind

(from *Szárazvillám*, 1957)

Revenant

This was the table. Surface, and legs.
This the wire, the lamp.
There was a glass to hand. It's here
This was the water. And I drank it.

And I looked out the window.
And I saw: the mist fell aslant
the field of an evening,
a big heavenly willow dipped
into eclipsed waters,
and I looked out the window
and I had eyes. And I had arms.

Now I live round chairlegs,
reach the knee of objects.
Then I shouldered through a space.
And such birds, such space.
Like a flaming garland's

ruffled leaves, tearing, flaring
they flew, muttering in swarms,
riven by a pulse
as if a heart split,
flew into birdbits —
That was the fire. That was the sky.

I leave. I'd finger
the floorboard, if I could.
Draughty. I dodge
in the street. I am not.

—Translated from the Hungarian by Hugh Maxton

(from *Napforduló*, 1967)

The Sleeping Horsemen

to Lajos Kassáck

December. Noon. Eye-scorching
snowfield broad as a hillside.
On the flat slope a heap of flagstone.
On its round edges
a hot, white, snowsheet:
a small pile of sleeping Bedouins.

What faces are these that bend
groundward, dark shrubs,
in this inverted sculptural group?
What dried-up, black
root-features, what
hot, dark breathing —

And deep down under the shore
what kind of Bedouin horses,
their shapes here and there heaving,
as inside the stable corridors,
silently, invisibly, they paw,
and their root-bearded large manes
begin to sway underground —

And what is this motion when
on the hot earth-horses' backs
the earthy brown trunks stretch,
leafy-haired, higher and higher,
and with one slow stupendous leap
spring out.

—*Translated from the Hungarian by Bruce Berlind*

(from *Napforduló*, 1967)

Between

The great sleeves of air,
air on which the bird
and the science of birds bear
themselves, wings on the fraying argument;
incalculable result
of a moment's leafy silhouette
bark and branch of a haze living upwards
like desire into the upper leaves
to inhale every three seconds
those big, frosty angels.

Downweight. On the plain
the mountain's motionless shocks
as they lie or kneel
peaks and escarpments,
geology's figure-sculpture,
the glen's a moment's distraction
and once more the forms and rocks,
chalky bone to outline
into identity of pleated stone.

Between the sky and the earth.

Creaking of rocks. As
the sun's clear ores
into themselves almost, stone into metal, as
a creature steps on in his claws smoke,
and up above the escarpment
ribbons of burning hoof,

then night in the desert, night as
quenching and reaching
its stony core, night below zero, and as
the tendons, joints, plaques

split and tear, as
they are strained in endless
splitting ecstasy
by routine dumb lightning
in black and white —

Between the day and the night.

Aches and stabbings,
visions, voiceless aquaducts,
inarticulate risings,
unbearable tension
of verticals between up and down.

Climates. Conditions.
Between. Stone. Tanktraces.
A strip of black reed rimming the plain
written in two lines, in the lake, the sky,
two black plaques of signsystem,
diacritic on the stars —

Between the sky and the sky.

—Translated from the Hungarian by Hugh Maxton

(from *Napforduló*, 1967)

Statues

Bitter.
          It was bitter, the sea, when
I rolled through the rock-throat down
a spiral staircase. A shingle, I spun,
behind me the hum of snail-shell
like memory in an abandoned house,
I rattled
like a skullfull of shrapnel.

Then I rumbled out onto the beach.
And there were the statues.

On a pedestal
a leather-covered tortoise-egg:
my skull boiled boiled in the sun,
my white helmet rolled away
a bubble on the sand,
I was lying down, my shoulder against a rock,
in filthy filthy white array.

Whose is this hunk?
Who was it, from a mountainous shale-chunk
with monstrous passion hacked
this indifference out?

And the plates of sheet-iron on me, the sheet-iron.
Banged-up boxes,
as they reflected their stammering light,
—a plane-wreck glitters like this,
but inside what stirs still lives,
a smatter of blood on the watchstrap,—
I lay smeared out on the rock,
life—the filth of it—on a stone.

Nothing more stubborn, more stubborn,
you fling yourself into a stone,
fling into a thing, fling into a stone
your living neck,
it's already a stone season,
its switched-off life half-blind,
who sculpted this indifference?
who was it, from a mountainous shale-chunk
chiseled your living neck?

Salt and sand and above them the rock-hunk,
gouged out cave-like in the sky,
this relative eternity,
this half-light of minerals—

the water murmurs, murmurs, its bed an Earth:
bitterness in a stone cask.

—Translated from the Hungarian by Bruce Berlind

(from *Napforduló*, 1967)

Akhenaton in Heaven

All these things there are the same. The mine.
A mountainside torn to the foot. Implements.
As he touches the limestone
the dawn's uncertain.
As if dawning from inside,
on the rock's thin face,
and stone and iron transparent
as after an ultimate disfunction.

There the forest.
The fog walks about in fragments.
Five-fingered, like abandoned hands
or hands that stretch up vertical,
a motion almost of traction
and yet of not reaching their meaning,
they float palely to the ground
as they trail —
as they expand and tumble,
vaporous, attenuated trunks,
another forest walks among the trees
and drives another foliage.

A tunnel under the trees.
Dark grass, gravel:
a set of narrow-gauge lines, at daybreak.
The sun is coming now, steaming,
piercing the fogs at a lateral angel,
mute rumbling recurs,
metal in the grass sparkles,
morning sparkles,
till suddenly a hedge springs up
for the lines end there in the grass.
Beyond, just a few sleepers
like unsteady steps ahead —
on the clearing the sun stays.

Fore-noon. Great plants.
The great camomile meadow is still,
pieces of iron in it,
honeycomb density over it,
white-spoked plants the suns
white galaxy without waves and no wind.
Always. For ever. Noon.

—Translated from the Hungarian by Hugh Maxton

(from *Napforduló*, 1967)

PERMISSIONS

"Revenant," "Between," and "Akhenaton in Heaven"
Reprinted from *Between: Selected Poems of Ágnes Nemes Nagy*, trans. by Hugh Maxton (Budapest: Corvina, 1989). Copyright ©Hugh Maxton. Reprinted by permission of William McCormack.

"The Sleeping Horsemen" and "To a Poet"
Reprinted from *Selected Poems*, trans. by Bruce Berlind (Iowa City: University of Iowa, 1980). Copyright ©1980 by the International Writing Program. Reprinted by Permision of the University of Iowa.

Amelia Rosselli [Italy]
1930–1996

The daughter of an Italian father and an English mother, Rosselli was born in Paris in 1930, and spent her childhood in France. Growing up speaking French, English and Italian, Rosselli was, from her childhood on, multilingual, which would highly influence the syntatical complexity of her poetry.

The second determining factor of her life was the murder of her father, the anti-Fascist martyr Carlo Rosselli, and her brother—both brutally killed by order of Benito Mussolini and Galeazzo Ciano, at Bagnole-de-l'Orne, Normandy. This event, and its aftermath—during the war she and her mother traveled throughout Europe to escape the Nazis—would have a lasting effect on her mental health. Much of her life was spent in therapy, and in 1996 she leaped from her high-rise apartment to her death. Rosselli herself has described the death of her father leaving an emotional void, which she attempted to fill through her writing.

After the war, she and her mother returned to Italy, staying for a short while in Florence before moving by herself to England, where she studied music: violin, piano, and composition. The following year, her mother died in Florence, and Amelia was forced, at eighteen years of age, to find self-employment. She began as a translator for Comunità in Rome. And here, directed by her father's cousin, Alberto Pincherle (who wrote under the name of Alberto Moravia), she began reading Italian writers while continuing to study music in her spare time. During these years, she also met the Italian poet Rocco Scotellaro at meeting of resistance partisans. They would remain close friends until his early death in 1953.

Influenced by writers such as Giuseppe Ungaretti, Cesare Pavese, Sandro Penna, and Eugenio Montale, Rosselli began moving toward literature as a career. In the late 1950s she was already writing some of her earliest lyrics, some of which were to be included in her two major early books, *Variazioni belliche* (1964, War Variations) and *Serie ospedaliera* (1969, Hospital Series). These two early works were championed by Pasolini and others. Her third major collection, *Documento, 1966–1973*, published in 1976, was followed by a hiatus from poetry for several years, until she published *Impromptu* (1981) and *Appunti sparsi e persi* (1983). Rosselli also composed experimental musical compositions of *musica concreta*.

BOOKS OF POETRY :

24 poesie (Turin: Einaudi, 1963); *Variazioni belliche* (Milan: Garzanti, 1964); *Serie ospedaliera* (Milan: Saggiatore, 1969); *Documento, 1966–1973* (Milan: Garzanti, 1976); *Primi scritti, 1952–1963* (Milan: Guanda, 1980); *Impromptu* (Genoa: San Marco dei Giustiniani, 1981); *Appunti sparsi e persi* (Reggio Emilia: Aelia Laelia, 1983); *La Libellula* (Genoa: SE, 1985); *Antologia poetica*, edited by Giacinto Spagnoletti (Milan: Garzanti, 1987).

ENGLISH LANGUAGE TRANSLATIONS:

Selections in *Shearsmen of Sorts: Italian Poetry 1975–1993*, edited by Luigi Ballerini (Forum Italicum Supplement, 1992) and in *The Promised Land: Italian Poetry After 1975*, edited by Luigi Ballerini, Beppe Cavatorta, Elena Coda and Paul Vangelisti (Los Angeles: Sun & Moon Press, 1999).

Poems from *War Variations*

Roberto, mother calls out, playfully rocking on the white
divan. I do not know
what God wants of me, serious
intentions rending eternity, or the frank laughter
of the puppet hanging from
the railing, railing yes, railing no, oh
postpone your heartfelt prayer with
a moving babble; car the dry and yellow leaves ravish
the wind that stirs them. Black vision tree that tends
toward the supreme power (pasture) which in fact I
think bleaches instead the ground beneath my feet, you are
my lover if the sky darkens, and the shiver
is yours, in the eternal forest. Empty city, full city, city
that soothes the fantastic for
the most part pain of the senses, you sit
sweltering after the meal you made of me, toy of levelling wind
from the coast I no longer dare
to face, I fear the red wave
of actually living, and the plants that say goodbye. Tom-
boy I straddle your bridges, and make them maybe
my own
nature.
I no longer know
who comes and who goes, let
delirium transform you into a senseless
gaming table, and the wild broom (room) faces out
spreading your sun across the reflecting glass.

*

    I was, I flew, I fell trembling into the
arms of God, and may this last sigh
be my whole being, and may the wave reward,
held in difficult union, my blood,
and from that supreme deceit may death
become vermilion be given back to me, and I
who from the passionate brawls of my comrades plucked
that longing for death
will enjoy, finally—the age of reason;
and may all the white flowers along the shore, and
all the weight of God
beat upon my prisons.

*

What is it with my heart that beats so softly
and desperate makes, maketh
the hardest soundings? you Those
tutories that I imprinted on afore he
tormented himself so
fiercely, and are vanished for him! O if mye
rabbits coursing throughthe nervies he for
frosty canals of my lymph (o life)
they don't stop, then yes, tha' I, me
yetsaclose to they dead! In all sinceauity my soul
may you remedy it, I ambrace you, you,—
may you find der Softe Worde, may you return
to the fathomed tongue that allows love to stay.

*

tomorrow's claws, ignite in deaf
whirlpools the lymph of your growth; don't
gothere; don't play with
your strength in the hell of wind and
hail today obliges your majesty to bow! If
you believe in the grammar of the poor, listen then to
the growing envy of the rich,—you will soon get used to
being born one of them.

*

And who can guarantee you are not one of those
who die on the shovel instead—who can warn
me of your spiderweb. Too late I
called the flies to shelter.

*

and what did that crowd want from my senses other than
my scorched defeat, or I who begged
to play with the gods and stumbled
like a poor whore up and down
the dark corridor—oh! wash my feet, take
the fierce accusations from my
bent head, bend

your accusations and undo all
my cowardice!: it wasn't my wish to break the delicate layer of ice
not my wish to break the mounting battle, no, I swear, it wasn't my
wish to break through your laughable
laughter!—but the hail has other reasons than
serving and the wet eastern wind of
evening does not dream of standing
watch by my
disenchanged lion sobs: no longer will I run
after every passage of beauty,—beauty is defeated, never again
at attention will I snuff out that fire now glimmering like
an old tree trunk
in which hollow swallows make nonsensical nests, child's play,
unreckoning misery, unreckoning misery of sympathy.

*

That violent rustling of birds, their flirtatious
rising in swarms from the hardest trees
(the tender lion roars in a flight of thought
and my faith lights up) their perching on the thinnest tops
their distracted gazing into the distance, *this*
is your desire, flying over my moutains of anxiousness
this is your warm thread of unknowing
anxiousness.

*

Inside of grace the number of my friends increased
and joy wove stories of impossible loves. Inside of
grace the poor tormented the rich and the hat was lifted
in an act of pure gratitude. Inside of Tao boredom vanished
outside of grace the murdered poet rhymed. Inside of
grace the passing bird dirtied the furniture
yesterday the day before yesterday there was a compass, today
the rain sadly pours and the promises of the rich are
a light that does not add up. Close to grace lay
love inside of grace every flower looked bad and at dawn
hell dirtied every light. Outside fury a hurricane
sinisterly scoured the main avenue of all our
frenzies. Such is the birth—such is the revenge of
the poor in spirit. Against the spirit of mercy
arose unanimous my salacious heart that came down touched

by grace but was unable to find the daytime sun except
in a cry of business. To find Chaos again a clarinet's
note was enough. (Indifference itself.)

*

We count endless dead! the dance is almost over! death,
the explosion, the swallow lying wounded on the ground, disease,
and hardship, poverty and the devil are my cases of
dynamite. Late I arrived to pity—late I lay among
bills in the pocket troubled by a peace that was not offered.
Near death the ground returned to the collectors the price
of glory. Late he lay on the ground that returned his blood
soaked with tears peace. Christ sitting on the ground on
reclined legs also lay in blood when Mary labored
with him.

Born in Paris labored in the epos of our flawed
generation. Lay in America among the rich fields of landlords
and of the stately State. Lived in Italy, barbaric country.
Fled from England, country of sophisticates. Hopeful
in the West where for now nothing grows.

The bamboo-café was the night.

The congenitals' tendency to goodness awakening.

*

The hell of light was love. The hell of love
was sex. The world's hell was the oblivion of the
simple rules of life: stamped paper and a simple
protocol. Four beds face down on the bed four
friends dead with a gun in their hand four keys
on the piano that give back hope.

—*Translated from the Italian by Lucia Re and Paul Vangelisti*

(from *Variazioni belliche*, 1964)

from *Serie Ospedaliera*

I sell you my cooking stove, then you scratch it
and sit unprepared on the desk
if I sell you the light yoke of
my diseased mind, the less stuff I have, the
happier I am. Undone by the rain
and by sorrows immeasurable menstruation
senility approaching, petroleum
imagination.

*

Searching for an answer to an unconscious voice
or believing, through it one's found it—I saw the muses
dazzled, spreading empty veils on their hands
not correcting themselves at the portal. Searching for
an answer to reveal, the orgiastic meaning of events
the particular obfuscation of a fate
that through brief rips of light opposes—the only sense
this prestigious act: that does not forget, lets
the walls graze the skin, suffers no estrangements
and does no revolt, against this shattering
and sobbing hurt, that is my moon on the face
the smell of angels on the arms, the step firm
and not concealed: the ruin slow but complete:
a non-detachment from low things, writing of them
supine.

—*Translated from the Italian by Lucia Re and Paul Vangelisti*

(from *Serie Ospedaliera*, 1969)

from *Documento (1966–1973)*

The angels exit
white and blue
and I sit at the balcony
black and white

Crisis of bovarysm
crisis of impoverishment!
crisis of flowers
crisis of workers

Dialogue is done in four
like a diagonal line
I describe buses
I start up again
more prayers
why are the trees blue?

(Things themselves
sow my heart with light)

*

As if I knew what the opposite means
things quite remote in the small homeland
outside the forest, and from the tropical heaps
in the beige of the tricolor
morgana with uncorrupted wings
in the poverty turned by now into a horrid kennel
victim that perpetuates her pain
as if truth were reborn from this clash
with the putrid air of these lost faces
in the unromantic hour of the very late morning
what if now you said
what is not conveniently said
in poetry?

—*Translated from the Italian by Lucia Re and Paul Vangelisti*

(from *Documento [1966–1973]*)

from *Impromptu*

When on a tank I get close
to that which was a tango, if

mercy was with me
when I won, or instead

if the late night were not
now the morning hour, I would

no longer write these beautiful
notes!—You really torture me?
and really teach me not to
torture the agonizing mind

of others without agony, though
missing in the sun of all the

splendid money you recognized
in that Capital of vice

that was Rome? And you ash-tree
o long brother of once
called Pierpaolo, a memory

is all I have of your vainglories
as if at bottom ambition were

to cast the last look
from the last bridge.

—Translated from the Italian by Lucia Re and Paul Vangelisti

(from *Impromptu*, 1981)

Rocco Scotellaro [Italy]
1923–1953

Rocco Scotellaro, born in 1923 at Tricarico (Matera), was one of the more actively involved of Italy's political poets. After World War II, at the age of 23, he became his village's first mayor, and was jailed in 1950 for his socialist activities. He resigned as mayor after serving the brief prison sentence, and left his home town to study more fully the conditions of the agrarian South. This research resulted in *Contadini del Sud*, a book on the Southern land problem in which peasants relate their stories to the author.

Scotellaro died near Naples in 1953. In 1954 Mondadori published his *È fatto giorno*, edited and introduced by Carlo Levi. *La poesia di Scotellaro*, edited by Franco Fortini, was published in 1974. During Scotellaro's last years, he worked on *L'uva puttanella*, a series of stories with peasant settings. —Paul Vangelisti

BOOKS OF POETRY:

È fatto giorno, ed. by Carlo Levi (Milan: Mondadori, 1954); *La poesia di Scotellaro*, ed. by Franco Fortini (Roma-Matera: Basilicata, 1974).

ENGLISH LANGUAGE TRANSLATIONS:

The Sky with Its Mouth Wide Open, trans. by Paul Vangelisti (Los Angeles: The Red Hill Press, 1976); *The Dawn Is Always New*, trans. by Ruth Feldman and Brian Swann (Princeton: Princeton University Press, 1980).

The Fathers of the Land If They Hear Us Singing

You sing, but what do you sing?
Don't disturb the fathers of the land.
The thirteen witches of the towns
have come together here in the evening.
And only a drunk sings the pleasure
of our disgrace.
And he alone can feel like a master
on this dead streetcorner.
We know how to beat the odds
as long as the narcosis
in a quart of wine holds out,
if the knife of incantation
repells the cloud's veil
over the woods of turkey oak,
if the fields drive away
the sultry wind that's risen.

But meanwhile the cobblestones
drown in the deep valley,
the little children want to gather
the confetti of hail
on the balconies.
The hail is the trophy
of the malicious saints of June
and we are the little children
their allies
given so much to smiling
on this beaten land.

But the heroes don't hunch over this way
with our wretched song.
In our fathers the grudge will last a long time.
Tomorrow we will be driven from our land,
but our fathers they know how to wait
for the day of justice.
Each will accuse. Each will have a say
even the old woman bleached by the flash of lightning:
in the doorway she whistled prayers
for the earth around her house.

—Translated from the Italian by Paul Vangelisti

(from *È fatto giorno*, 1954)

The Graves the Houses

The graves the houses...
heart heart
don't stop beating.
The smoke of chimneys
in the damp air;
the footstep of enemies:
they beat on your very door.
Heart heart
don't stop beating.
The graves the houses,
November has come,
the churchbell: it's high noon,
it's a trick of the weather.
The dead cannot see,
mother is blind at the fireside.
Heart heart
don't stop beating.
The graves the houses
say goodbye and send
love back to the other evening.
Like flies dying on the windows
the prisoners run to the gates,
it's always slammed shut the horizon.
How many have nothing but hope!
heart, don't stop beating.
The graves the houses,
it's the 10th of August
that we were evicted.
What are they doing where we lived?
Are the keys turning in hotels?
The miserable, the good
are they damned to removal?
The Jewish women wail on the stones
of the ruined temple.
How many have nothing but prayer!
heart, don't stop beating.
The graves the houses,
stooped men, shrunken women
they confess at the windows
of the National Lottery.
My soul

is in this breath
which fills and empties me.
What will become of me?
What will become of us?
For him who will walk
from the graves to the houses
from the houses to the graves
shouting into the mineshafts
shouting at the miners
heart, don't stop beating.

—Translated from the Italian by Paul Vangelisti

(from *È fatto giorno*, 1954)

The Sky with Its Mouth Wide Open

At this hour the wind is caught
in the ravine along the Basento.
And the mountains vanish.
And the sky is stuck with its mouth wide open.
We see a little girl in the chicken coop
above the Murge of Pietrapertosa.
Who hears the sandstone which crumbles
all at once on our backs?
the rustle of a serpent
the train in the valley?
Everyone is faithful to his job.
Two bitches down in the flats
have flushed a rabbit. It flees
like a spirit recognized.

(1945)

—Translated from the Italian by Paul Vangelisti

(from *È fatto giorno*, 1954)

You Don't Put Us to Sleep Hopeless Cuckoo

All about the brown mountains
your color is swelling
September friend of my street.
You are hunted in our midst,
they heard you near our women
when shipwrecked crickets
out of the burnt stubble
rose up to our doors with a cry.
And there are branches of dried figs
and green tomatoes under the roof
and a sack of hard grain, a heap
of crushed almonds.

You don't put us to sleep
hopeless cuckoo,
with you call:
Yes, we will give our steps back to the paths,
we will go back to our struggles tomorrow
that the streams are once again yellow
in the gullies
and wind ruffles
the shawls in the closets.

(1947)

—Translated from the Italian by Paul Vangelisti

(from È fatto giorno, 1954)

A House Behind the Prison Cypress

Turtle-dove, don't show yourself
in a soft sea-green blouse,
the flowers are still in the leaves
and the bark is slow to whisper.

My prison, lavish gate,
sea of voices squeezed into a ring
swell for you in harmony
turtle-dove who plays Ondine

among the cypress branches.
In the air trembling is the light, the houses...
and all of it seems unreal,
but you know with your beak
how to probe my heart.
But we have no more songs,
we sang them all
day and night at your balcony.

(1950)

—Translated from the Italian by Paul Vangelisti

(from *È fatto giorno*, 1954)

Economics Lesson

I asked you one day who posted
the sentinels of spruce
up there in the Dolomites.
I asked you many other things
of the rock rose, of myrtle,
of the gummy inula,
names of nothing to do with economy.
You answered me
that a father who loves his children
can only watch them go away.

(1952)

—Translated from the Italian by Paul Vangelisti

(from *È fatto giorno*, 1954)

Takahashi Mutsuo [Japan]
1937

Born in Yahata, Kyushu in 1937, Takahashi Mutsuo spent most of his early youth with relatives and other families, his father having died soon after his birth. With the end of World War II, he began to write poetry, publishing his first book of poetry, *Mino, My Bull*, in 1959. During that same period Takahashi became friends with Friar Tsuda, and became interested in Catholicism. He graduated from Fakuoka University of Education in 1962.

From the beginning, Takahashi's poetry was overtly homosexual, and his second book, *Rose Tree, Fake Lovers*, published in 1964, has been compared to the writings of Walt Whitman and Allen Ginsberg. That same year, he became acquainted with Japanese novelist, Mishima Yukio, with whom he was to remain friendly until Mishima's suicide in 1970.

Over the next several years, Takahashi published numerous books of poetry, fiction, and essays, including *Dirty Ones, Do Dirtier Things, Twelves Perspective, Ode, Holy Triangle,* and *King of the Calendar.* He also traveled extensively, staying for more than a month in New York City in 1971 and for briefer periods in Israel, Turkey, Greece, Italy, France, Belgium, England, Mexico, Korea, Spain, Morocco, Portugal, Taiwan and other countries throughout the world. His work has been translated into many languages.

In the 1970s Takahashi worked with translations of Greek and French literature, published a magazine, *Symposium,* and continued his travels, this time to San Francisco, Germany, Austria, Hong Kong, and Algeria. In 1982 he received the 20th Rekitei Prize for his collection of poetry, *The Structure of the Kingdom.* The same year, he published *A Bunch of Keys.*

Other prizes include the Takami Jun Prize for *Usagi no Niwa* (The Garden of Rabbits), the Yomiuri Literary Prize for his haiku and tanka *Keiko Onjiki* (Practice/Drinking Eating), the Gendai-shi Hanatsubaki (Modern Poetry Flowering Camellia) Prize for *Tabi no E: Imagines Itineris* (Pictures from a Journey), and the Nihon Gendai Shiika Bungakukan (Museum of Modern Japanese Verse) Prize for *Ane no Shima* (Older Sister's Island).

BOOKS OF POETRY:

Mino, Atashi no Oushi (Tokyo: Sabaku Shijin Shūdan Jimukyoku, 1959); *Bara no Ki, Nise no Koibito-tachi* (Tokyo: Gendaishi Kōbō, 1964); *Nemuri to Okashi to Rakka to* (Tokyo: Sōgetsu Art Center, 1965); *Yogoretaru Mono wa Sarani Yogoretaru Koto o Nase* (Tokyo: Shichōsha, 1966); *Takahashi Mutsuo Shishū* (Tokyo: Shichōsha, 1969); *Homeuta* (Tokyo: Shichōsha, 1971); *Koyomi no Ô: Rex Fastorum* (Tokyo: Shichōsha, 1972); *Kyūku chō* [haiku] (Tokyo: yukawa Shobō 1973); *Dōshi I* (Tokyo: Shichōsha, 1974); *Watakushi* (Tokyo: Ringo-ya, 1975); *Kōdō Shō* [haiku] (Tokyo: Ringo-ya, 1977); *Michi no Ae* (with *Kyūka-Chō*) [tanka] (Tokyo: Ringo-ya, 1978); *Dōshi II* (Tokyo: Shichōsha, 1978); *Sasurai to iu Na no Chi nite* (Tokyo: Shoshi Yamada, 1979); *Shinsen Takahashi Mutsuo Shishū* (Tokyo: Shichōsha, 1980); *Okoku no Kōzō* (Tokyo: Ozawa Shoten, 1975);

Kagitaba (Toyko: Shoshi Yamada, 1982); *Bunkōki: Prismatica* (Tokyo: Shichōsha, 1985); *Usagi no Niwa* (Tokyo: Shoshi Yamada, 1987); *Keiko Onjiki* [haiku and tanka] (Tokyo: Zenzaikutsu, 1987); *Tabi no E: Imagines Itineris* (Toyko: Shoshi Yamada, 1992); *Nii-makura* [tanka] (Tokyo: Shichōsha, 1992); *Kanazawa Hyakku, Kanazawa Hyakkei* [haiku] (Tokyo: Chikuma Shobō, 1993); *Zoku: Takahashi Mutsuo Shishū* (Tokyo: Shichōsha, 1995); *Ane no Shima* (Tokyo: Shūeisha, 1995); *Tamamono* (Tokyo: Seikoku Sho'oku, 1998); *Kono Yo aruiha Hakono Hito* (Tokyo: Shichōsha, 1998).

ENGLISH LANGUAGE TRANSLATIONS:

Poems of a Penisist, trans. by Hiroaki Sato (Chicago: Chicago Review Press, 1975); *A Bunch of Keys*, trans. by Hiroaki Sato (Trumansburg, New York: The Crossing Press, 1984); *Sleeping, Sinning, Falling*, trans. by Hiroaki Sato (San Francisco: City Lights, 1992); *Voice Garden: Selected Poems by Mutsuo Takahashi*, trans. by Hiroaki Sato (Tokyo: Star Valley Library, 1996).

Mino

Mino
My bull
Before I reached your knees
I was already your sister
I climbed your sturdy legs
Or from between your crescent-shaped horns
I looked at the distant ocean
From field to field where the wind blazes
We ran together
You brandishing your horns
I streaming my hair behind me
At night we slept, holding each other
Belly to belly, thigh to thigh
Until the terrible sunrise

—*Translated from the Japanese by Hiroaki Sato*

(from *Mino, Watashi no Oushi*, 1959)

To a Boy

Boy,
you are a hidden watering place under the trees
where, as the day darkens, gentle beasts with calm eyes
appear one after another.

Even if the sun drops flaming at the end of the fields where grass stirs greenly
and a wind pregnant with coolness and night-dew agitates your leafy bush,
it is only a premonition.

The tree of solitude that soars with ferocity,
crowned with a swirling night,
still continues to sleep in your dark place.

—*Translated from the Japanese by Hiroaki Sato*

(from *Sasurai to iu Na no Chi nite*, 1979 [poems from 1958–1961])

At a Throat

Fury—iron swung down,
then, black fleeing in many blue nights.
For a while through the trees your face, now a pulpy mess, chased me,
closed eyelashes trembling as if they wanted to say something.
But I no longer envy your gentle throat.
What has come between you and me:
an act, a crime—and, time.
                    Hot morning, throat gurgling,
I drink water. Sweat turns into beads, blankets my forehead, and trembles.
Reflected in the sweat beads, a breeze from a tamarisk is trembling.
I take a plow in my arms of solitude and, in the deep noon, become a man.
That pitiful fellow—I divide the coarse soil into two strands of soil
and, back turned to the noon where silence resounds, and plowing,
walk step by step toward the evening with lightning flaring in the clouds.
—In the barn's cold darkness gleams a razor-sharp sickle.

—*Translated from the Japanese by Hiroaki Sato*

(from *Sasurai to iu Na no Chi nite*, 1979 [poems from 1958–1961])

Foreskin (from *Ode*)

FORESKIN
And with the tongue tip sharpened like a needle, everts the wrapping cloth
A bandage wound tightly round and round the ring finger
The bandages for an abscess, the bandages rolling up a fireman burned all over
The bandages that wrap the invisible man, the bandages with a mummified boy-
     king sleeping in them
The white cover-cloth a leper has pulled over himself, from head to toe
The flowering stalk of a butterbur, a peapod, skin-covers of a bamboo shoot
A miscanthus roll, a taffy in a bamboo leaf, a butterball wrapped in cellophane
A hat, the Pope's miter, a cardinal's hat, the hood for a child in the snow
     country
The chef's somewhat grimy white toque
The KKK hood, socks, a rubber thimble
A rubber glove everted like a pelt of gelatin
A god's glove that has fallen from heaven toward the sea of chaos
A turban, a calpec, the hood of the Eskimo parka
Roofs rising in the Kremlin, in rows as if in a fairy tale
In the Kremlin, from the balcony

Soviet elders wave to May Day crowds in Red Square
All in uniform caps
At Buckingham Palace, guards swagger in bearskins
Pericles' helmet, Napolean's hat
The Pohai Emperor's hat, the Egyptian priest's headdress
The Old Blossomer's cap, Mr. Ebisu's cap
The fearful shoes, the shoes that, once put on, can't be removed
The rubber boots worn by a young cock in the fish market
The riding boots made to fit the legs closely
Each time the rider walks its spurs clack, clack
A hill-fresh yam wearing a maxicoat
A wandering yakuza's slightly soiled cape
A man rolled in a mattress carried by thugs to be dumped in the river
One unhooks the beltless, pulls the zipper
And recklessly pulls down the pants
A gaiter unwound swiftly, the leather chaps
A shutter pulled down with a rattle, a curtain, a double-leaf louver door
Concealing a man, panting, his hairy shins showing, a surgical intern in white
A noncommissioned officer's cap pulled down to the eyes, his uniform well-creased
The armor hiding the young blond knight, his Lordship
On a morning when each exhaled breath visibly turns into steam, white misty
    droplets
An auto repairman's one-piece workwear
The zipper extending down its stained cloth from neck to crotch
When one pulls it down in one breath
There, vividly, jumps out the young flesh, flushed with cold—
The leaping pink flesh wrapped in a lobster shell
The pelty diving suit, a suede suit
Skinned with a stone and bloody, a wild animal pelt
An antelope, a wolf, a coyote, their pelts
The membrane that wraps the bloody heart of a wild animal
The membrane of the morning haze that wraps the bloody daybreak

—*Translated from the Japanese by Hiroaki Sato*

(from *Homeuta*, 1971)

Myself in the Manner of a Suicide

I will be buried in the road, cut far off from my right hand.
(Because of its behavior the right hand is forever cursed.)
Among the roads, a road with particularly heavy traffic of carts and horses.
Endlessly crisscrossed by the ruts that come and go,
my face will have deep wrinkles imitating agony chiseled into it.
My flesh will rot like a seed potato and, rotting, become transparent;
but because, blocked by the hard surface of the road, it cannot sprout,
in the dark earth my face, my phallus, will meaninglessly multiply.
Rather, from the sinful hand that was cut off and buried
I will bud as a new plant,
but the multiplying me in the earth will never take part in it.
I will become a single tree, spread in the light,
and as a testimony to my self putrefying in the earth, to my self that was once in the
     sunlight,
will flutter, and blaze, in one spot in the ravaged landscape.
Of that dark blazing face of that dark blazing day,
I now exist as a clumsy copy.

    —Translated from the Japanese by Hiroaki Sato

(from *Watakushi*, 1971)

Myself with Cheese

As an embodiment of the word "manducation," for example
there will be a hunk of cheese with a golden fragrance.
If, to spotlight the manner of its golden embodiment,
the plate on which the hunk of cheese is placed is an ordinary plate of tin,
and where the tin plate is a casual wood table,
what will be the manner of my being with knife in hand, in front of the table?
I, as poet, witness this embodiment of gold.
Because it is said that to witness as poet
must be more impersonal than to witness as eater,
before the plate of cheese, my beard is an impersonal beard,
my wet teeth and tongue are impersonal teeth and tongue,
even the lifted knife is an impersonal knife.

    —Translated from the Japanese by Hiroaki Sato

(from *Watakushi*, 1971)

Myself in the Manner of a Troubador

Mounting a horse with an abundant mane and in glittery armor, a hero
will have to have a face as dazzling as that orb of day.
But a base one ordered to sing of heroes,
I cannot have a face, however ordinary.

Like a photo of the hateful man an abandoned woman tore into shreds,
my face is torn apart and lost in advance.
Faceless, holding in both hands a lyre quite like a face,
on a hill with a view of the field shining with battle dust, under a plane tree,

or on a boulder of a cape overlooking the sea where triremes come and go,
I sit for thousands of years, I just continue to sit.
The odes that, faceless, I sing in praise of passing heroes
overflow as beautiful blood from the chest wound I hide with the lyre.

—*Translated from the Japanese by Hiroaki Sato*

(from *Watakushi*, 1975)

Myself as in the Onan Legend

My face will be dark.
The glittering liquid that spurts out of my holy procreative center
will not be received into that contractile interior, which is eternally female,
but spill, and keep spilling, on the cold lifeless ground,
so my sons, who are my shadow, will as Little Leeches make a round of the earth,
make a round of the water labyrinth at the bottom of the earth, make a round of
   the crisscross paths inside the tree,
and, ejected from the skyward mouth of every leaf at the tip of the tree,
will drift aimlessly in the empty blue sky and become lost,
so my face should have been what my sons of the endlessly continuing
glittering links of light began to weave and ended weaving,
so the overflowing light is behind me, not before me.
My face, the whole face as one large mouth of darkness,
in the overflowing, spilling light, is voicelessly shouting.

—*Translated from the Japanese by Hiroaki Sato*

(from *Watakushi*, 1975)

Three Curses for Those to Be Born

"Be Afraid of Fish"
Be afraid of fish.
Be afraid of fish that have no voice.
Be afraid of fish that are soul-shaped.
Be afraid of fish that are the alphabet at the bottom of man's memory.
Be afraid of fish that are more aged than man or tortoise.
Be afraid of fish that came into being when water did.
Be afraid of fish that know every strand of bog moss, yet keep silent about it.
Be afraid of fish that are more shadowy than the shadow in the water which is more
     dreamy than the dream.
Be afraid of fish that silently slip in and out of your nightly dream.
Be afraid of fish that remain in the water even when they mate.
Be afraid of fish whose gills continue to move even while alseep.
Be afraid of fish that move their mouths, afloat, with their air bladders, in watery
     heaven.
Be afraid of fish that are softer than lovers when caught.
Be afraid of fish, the foul feeders, that swallowed a god's phallus that was twisted off
     and discarded.
Be afraid of fish that shed human tears when broiled on fire.
Be afraid of fish that are your fathers, that are your mothers.
Be afraid of fish that occupy your entirety the morning after you were bored by fish.
Be afraid of fish that remain fish-shaped even after turning into bones.
As for the fish bones, put them on your palms and return them to the water,
going down, barefoot, to the beach where your sewage pipe empties itself.

"Wheat King"
I am the Wheat King.
My dried-up small face is half rotten in the darkness of earth.
Extending, transparent and arched, from the black, cold putrefaction, are the buds of
     disease.
Feeling the air of early spring, the buds grow sparsely and turn pale as a dead man's
     brow.
When the wind becomes warm, the feeble wheat seedlings catch fever at once.
The ears of wheat, broiled with high fever and emaciated, are pulled off by women's
     violent thigh-like fingers.
and are slashed, slashed with flails all day long.
Stone mortars smash me, and when I become wheat flour of poor coloration, I'm put
     through sieves.
I am kneaded with water, baked in ovens, and, as shabby noodles, carried into mouths
     with rotten teeth.
The left-overs are thrown, with saliva, into vats, and are made to ferment grumblingly.

I become a coarse liquor, go down men's sinuous throats, and wander with their muddy
   blood.
I am disfigured life that is poured out from man into woman at the end of travels of
   sufferings.
I am great death that fills that disfigured life.
Take me from this seed pot.

   "Those with Wings"
Those with wings
those with long beaks
those that fly across clamorously moving their beaks up and down
those with pointed eyes
those that come and go between the city of life and the city of death
those that cross over both into purity and into filth
those that circle man's sky cautiously
those that, with scaly legs, alight on the sandy beach of time
those that clutch pebbles with crooked nails
those that stand about in flocks
those that ruffle up their feathers, vying for food laid out by the gods
those that are treacherous and easily surprised
those that flap up all at once
those that are bathed in overflowing scarlet as they dive into the sunset
those that chase the shooting stars
those that reach the shore of the spirits throughout the night
those that fly up, holding white-haired, wrinkled babies in their beaks
those that fly down, like frost, to the ridges of roofs in dawn
those that push orphan souls into the crotches of women sloppily asleep:
shoot those suspicious shadows.

   —*Translated from the Japanese by Hiroaki Sato*

(from *Kagitaba*, 1982)

On the Reality of the Pot

1
There is a pot.

2
The fact that there is a pot is not more certain than the certainty of the syntax that says
there is a pot.

3

To make factually certain that there is a pot, the position of the pot, for example, on the axis of co-ordinates may be set. For now, the pot is in the darkness. Definitely outside the line of vision of my, or your, wide open eyes.

4

It is probably useful also to limit the darkness. For example, a corner of a kitchen made by piling up cut stones, the space below a dangling bunch of garlic, the tip of a whisker of a Chinese cricket, a line of light from the skylight—also outside any of these.

5

Next, we make limits within the limits and set its positon in the darkness. Its ass on the oven built directly on the earthen floor (or rather by putting stones in the shape of !!), it has a wooden lid on top. "On top" means simply "facing the ceiling," but because the sheer darkness there doesn't reveal the ceiling, the upper-lower relations carry no meaning. (Of course, the space below the bunch of garlic, too, is meaningless, and the tip of a whisker of the Chinese cricket also becomes meaningless.)

6

This means that to say the vigorous tongue of fire is licking the tail of the pot from below is also meaningless. If the expression, "from below," is meaningless, the expression, "tail of the pot," naturally becomes meaningless. Because the tail exists as something opposed to the head and, in an upright being, the two imply upper-lower relations.

7

As long as upper-lower relations do not make sense, you can't necessarily say of fire that it's licking the pot. The expression, "The pot is licking the fire," won't be wrong, either.

8

Here, let us digress somewhat and anecdotally consider the fire. That the fire is coming out of the wood placed on the earthen floor is no more than one possible explanation. If, for example, we are to take into consideration the match which was the direct cause of the fire in this instance, it will be more appropriate to explain that there is a certain amount of time between the wood, which, because of the fire that came from elsewhere, is in the transitional process from wood to carbon (and ultimately to ash), and the pot. Of course, you must at the same time think of reversing the order of "*wood*" and *pot*" to "*pot*" and "*wood*."

9

Well, then, is it possible to say that the fire came from the match? It will be far more accurate to say that even with the match the fire came from elsewhere to it, no, to the space between the compound at the tip of the match-stick and the compound on the side of the match-box (match-stick and match-box may be reversed) and stayed at the tip of the matchstick for a certain amount of time.

10

If that is the case, where did the fire come from? Is it that in some invisible place there is the ideated world or hometown of fire and it has been called out to signal the friction between the tip of the match-stick and the side of the box? Or is it that one of the seeds of fire which are everywhere in the field of air has been made to sprout by a sudden stimulation? We will leave to the future the unknowability of this conjecture, as it is.

11

If we could make a transition from the uncertainty of the fire to the certainty of the pot, we certainly would be happy. No, it is fully possible that such happiness is no more than our wishful thinking.

12

At any rate, let's begin with the shape and the size of the pot. As for the shape, we will choose that of the traveler's hat of the ancient god of the road, the skull of the enemy commander which was also used as a wine cup at the victory banquet, the grave which the convict is forced to dig for himself, the mortar-shape of hell pictured in our imagination...in short, wide-mouthed, deep, and as conspicuously special-shaped as possible. As for the size, its diameter is about the length of the lower arm of an adult male. Its depth is approximately the length from the wrist to the elbow. But as something made by hand, the size is irregular. That is to say, both the diameter and the depth may differ slightly, depending on where you measure them.

13

If its shape and size are special, it is desirable that the material be also special. One would hope it is shoddy pig iron made by stepping on the foot-bellows and containing a good deal of impure elements. Therefore, it is on the whole thick and uneven. Because it has remained intimate with fire for at least a hundred fifty to sixty years in time (assuming there is time), the parts that are directly exposed to fire and the parts that aren't have changed differently: either thinning by heating or increasing in thickness through the attachment of soot. There are differences in parts, but on the whole it is as black as if the darkness around it had condensed. It may indeed be the condensed darkness, not "as if."

14

Let us continue for convenience. If, as we say conveniently, fire is burning outside, something is cooking inside. This is what's called logic. The most fragile fiction.

15

Something...like beans. Like oatmeal. Like overripe tomatoes. Like meat with bones....It may simply be water. Even the air. Or vacuum. Though it must be vacuum as substance.

16

Why are we concerned that it must be some substance? Because if the reality of the pot remains uncertain after all this description, we will want to make the certainty of what's in it guarantee the certainty of the container.

17

Still, if what's cooking is vacuum, the pig iron that is the material of the pot itself will cook and diminish in weight though only little by little. But wait. The pig iron may not be diminishing, but merely moving elsewhere. That will be the case, especially if the pig iron is a metaphor for the condensed darkness.

18

The darkness is a container. Rather, the notion of container starts out from the darkness. If your brain is thinking about the true nature of what's cooking in that darkness, what's cooking may well be your brain. Will you say the brain, too, is no more than a metaphor for the darkness?

19

There is a pot, we began. It could have been a shoe, a jute bag, an armory, a measure for wheat, a silkworm moth, a horse-bean pod, or any other thing.

20

Even so, we chose a pot over everything else, because a pot is thought to be extremely common and boringly certain. But, for now, we must pay attention to the point, "is thought." When it comes to where the pot, which is thought to be certain, came from, we must say that our conjecture is cast in the unknowable darkness, just like our conjecture on where the fire, which is thought to be uncertain, came from.

21

That there is a pot is that there is darkness. This is the same as saying we are. That is, the darkness called us has conjectured the reality or the unreality of the darkness called a pot. Or, the reverse of that.

—*Translated from the Japanese by Hiroaki Sato*

(from *Kagitaba*, 1982)

INDEX OF POEMS

RAFAEL ALBERTI   9
  "*The Cruel Angels*"   11
  "*False Angel*"   12
  "*The Dead Angels*"   13
  "*Soul in Torment*"   14
  "*Open Letter*"   15
  "*Buston Keaton Searches Through the Forest for His*
    Sweetheart, a Full-Blooded Cow"   17
  "*Goya*"   19
INGEBORG BACHMANN   23
  "*Paris*"   25
  "*Wood and Shavings*"   25
  "*Early Noon*"   26
  "*Tell Me, Love*"   28
  "*Black Waltz*"   29
  "*A Type of Loss*"   30
RUBÉN DARÍO   31
  "from *Thistles*"   33
  "*Towers of God! Poets!*"   33
  "*To Roosevelt*"   34
  "*Philosophy*"   36
  "*Life and Death*"   36
GÜNTER EICH   37
  "*Inventory*"   39
  "*Where I Live*"   40
  "*End of August*"   40
  "*Munch, Consul Sandberg*"   41
  "*For Example*"   41
  "*A Mixture of Routes*"   42
  "*Continuing the Conversation*"   44
GUNNAR EKELÖF   49
  "*Sonata Form Denatured Prose*"   51
  "*To Remember*"   51
  "*Sketch from the steppes*"   53
  "*Absentia animi*"   53
  "*Elegy*"   56
  "*Greece*"   57
J.V. FOIX   59
  "*Bring on the Oars...*"   61
  [*When I spied my rival*}   61
  "*Practice*"   61
  "*With Cold-Numbed Body...*"   63
  "*We Would Have Split More Pines if the Oxen*
    Hadn't Stared at Us So Fixedly"   65
  "*Beyond the Centuries, Immobile*"   65

ÁNGEL GONZÁLEZ 67
  "Before I Could Call Myself Ángel González" 69
  "Dogs Against the Moon" 69
  "Astonishing World" 70
  "Yesterday" 71
  "The Future" 72
  "Words Taken from a Painting by José Hernández" 74
JORGE GUILLÉN 77
  "The Hills" 79
  "Calm of Gardens" 79
  "The Names" 80
  "Federico García Lorca" 80
HAGIWARA SAKUTARŌ 84
  "Bamboo" 86
  "Bamboo" 86
  "Dish of Skylarks" 87
  "Death" 87
  "Frog's Death" 88
  "The Reason the Person Inside Looks Like a Deformed Invalid" 88
  "Chair" 89
  "Spring Night" 89
  "The World of Bacteria" 89
  "Lover of Love" 90
  "You Frog" 91
  "Skylark Nest" 91
  "Secret of the Garden of a Vacant House Seen in a Dream" 94
HAYASHI FUMIKO 95
  "Under the Lantern" 96
  "Taking Out the Liver" 96
  "Red Sails Gone to Sea" 97
  "Spread Out in the Sky the Cherry Tree Branches" 99
  "Stubborn, Strong" 100
  "I've Seen Fuji" 100
  "Early Evening Light" 101
  "The Fat Moon Has Vanished" 102
FRIGYES KARINTHY 104
  "The Message in the Bottle (The Poet Is Asked Why He No
    Longer Writes Poems)" 105
  "Dandelion" 106
  "Struggle for Life" 107
ARTHUR LUNDKVIST 109
  "To Maria" 111
  "Relativity" 111
  "The Wheel Book" 112
  from *Journeys in Dream and Imagination* 113
    [It is the dog returning...] 113
    [A gate, a gate!] 114
    [You can see flocks of birds...] 114

JACKSON MAC LOW 116
  Selections from *"The 11ᵗʰ of July"* 118
  "September Pack" 119
  "16th Dance—Being Red Enough—21 February 1964" 120
  "A Lack of Balance But Not Fatal" 121
  "Giant Otters" 132
OSIP MANDELSHTAM 125
  "Insomnia" 126
  "On Stony Pierian Spurs" 126
  [Can't remember how long] 127
  "I Am Deaf" 128
  "Leningrad" 129
  [For the thundering glory of years to come,] 129
  [The day was rearing its five heads...] 130
  [Charlie Chaplin/Stepped out of the cinema] 131
JOÃO CABRAL DE MELO NETO 133
  "Pirandello II" 135
  "Daily Space" 135
  "Within the Loss of Memory" 136
  "(Landscape of the Capibaribe River)" 136
  "Written with the Body" 139
  "Education by Stone" 143
HENRI MICHAUX 144
  "The Big Fight" 146
  "Insects" 146
  "Under the Obsessive Beacon of Fear" 147
  "The Village of Madmen" 147
  "In the Night" 148
  from *A Certain Plume* 149
  "On the Spit" 150
  from *Poetry for Power* 151
  "The Days, the Days, the End of Days" 153
O.V. DE L. MILOSZ 154
  "When she comes..." 155
  "Monkey Dance" 155
  "November Symphony" 156
  "Psalm of the King of Beauty" 157
  "Psalm of the Morning Star" 158
ÁGNES NEMES NAGY 159
  "To a Poet" 162
  "Revenant" 162
  "The Sleeping Horsemen" 163
  "Between" 164
  "Statues" 165
  "Akhenaton in Heaven" 167

AMELIA ROSSELLI 169
  from *War Variations* 170
    [Roberto, mother calls out...] 170
    [I was, I flew, I fell trembling into...] 170
    [What is it with my heart...] 171
    [tomorrow's claws...] 171
    [And who can guarantee you are not one...] 171
    [and what did that crowd want from my senses...] 171
    [That violent rustling of birds] 172
    [Inside of grace the number of my friends...] 172
    [We count the endless dead!] 173
    [The hell of light was love....] 173
  from *Serie Ospedaliera* 174
    [I sell you my cooking stove...] 174
    [Searching for an answer to an unconscious voice] 174
  from *Documento (1966–1973)* 174
    [The angels exit] 174
    [As if I knew what the opposite means] 175
  from *Impromptu* 175
    [When on a tank I get close] 175
ROCCO SCOTELLARO 177
  "The Fathers of the Land If They Hear Us Singing" 178
  "The Graves the Houses" 179
  "The Sky with Its Mouth Wide Open" 180
  "You Don't Put Us to Sleep Hopeless Cuckoo" 181
  "A House Behind the Prison Cypress" 181
  "Economics Lesson" 182
TAKAHASHI MUTSUO 183
  "Mino" 185
  "To a Boy" 185
  "At the Throat" 186
  "Foreskin" from *Ode* 186
  "Myself in a Manner of a Suicide" 188
  "Myself with Cheese" 188
  "Myself in the Manner of a Troubador" 189
  "Myself as in the Onan Legend" 189
  "Three Curses for Those to Be Born" 190
  "On the Reality of the Pot" 191